HISTORY OF NIGERIA

HISTORY OF NIGERIA

BABA OLU

WEST AFRICAN

The 'Purchase' of Nigeria

From the West Australian, July 5, 1899
ROYAL NIGER COMPANY - IMPERIAL PURCHASE OF NIGERIA.

LONDON, July 4.

The House of Commons yesterday by 223 votes to 101 agreed to the Vote of £865,000, with which it is pro-posed to purchase the rights of the Royal Niger Company in "West Africa."

Sir Michael Hicks-Beach, while praising the company's administration of the territories embraced in their charter, admitted that the Anglo-French relations in regard to West Africa since 1897 had been more strained than the public had appreciated.

Owing to the Royal Niger Company having had a free hand, a terrible war had been threatened. The Niger territories, now called Nigeria, have been administered by the Royal Niger Company under a Royal charter dated July 10, 1836. They cover about 500,000 square miles and contain a population variously estimated at from 20,000,000 to 40,000,000. In October last year it was reported that the Imperial Government had taken over Akassa from the company, and the terms upon which the territories were to be transferred to the Imperial Government have been made the subject of many rumors.[1]

F rom the Auckland Star. July 5, 1899
(More insight; Different payment amount reported; Same Outcome):

The wisdom and justice of allowing- companies established mainly for money-making purposes to make war upon native tribes and establish governments of an autocratic character over vast possessions of the Crown may well be questioned. The methods of some of these companies are not characterized by fine scruples, and whenever their interests conflict with those of the native tribes inhabiting the lands under their rule the black man receives scant justice.

So long as the wars arising out of the operations of these trading companies are confined to expeditions against bloodthirsty negro potentates the Home Government are not too inquisitive regarding the methods of warfare adopted, and the news received from time to time that thousands of blacks at some place in the African wilds have been mown down by Maxim guns served by a handful of British troops is usually hailed with popular acclamation as another evidence of our national prowess. But when the action of these chartered companies brings the empire into conflict with other European States which are. pursuing the same game then the matter assumes an entirely different complexion.

For several years past the Royal Niger Company has been beset by French encroachments on the North and West, and German operations on the East. The differences with Germany were easily settled owing- to the reasonable and amicable disposition manifested by the German Government, but France, in Nigeria, as in Egypt, has manifested a disposition to flout "perfidious Albion." Three or four agreements on the boundary question have been' made, but each one, so far as French claims went, left certain boundary lines in an indefinite state, and in a country over which the administration is of the loosest description, many parts being rarely' visited even by trading agents, it is easy for explorers and adventurers to enter, and on the. strength of treaties with native kings who have not the smallest notion of what they are signing to establish a basis for national claims. This has gone on for many years in Nigeria, to the great disturbance of friendly relations between England and France; the announcement, therefore, made some time ago that all outstanding' points of difference had been amicably settled was a relief.

To prevent future complications and also to strengthen Great Britain's hold over the Niger territories the Imperial Government have now resolved to purchase out the rights of the Chartered Company for £560,000. It seems a big price but is after all a trifle compared with the cost of a European war, which the Chancellor of the Exchequer declared had been more nearly threatened than the public appreciated through the free hand exercised by the company. [2]

Preface

Frederick Lugard, a dismissed English Army Officer seeking redemption and fame, had proved useful to Colonial ambitions as sanctioned, but unofficial armed muscle in Karonga (Malawi) and Buganda (Uganda) in East Africa, before his invitation to West Africa by the Royal Niger Company, where his style and ambition once again aligned with English colonial interests.

The West African frontier force, which was atimes under Lugard's direct control, gave him the leverage to pursue objectives, which were sometimes at odds with those of the more experienced colonial officials.

The (il)legal subjugation of self-sustaining countries and subsuming of these into the Berlin rendezvous-mapped Colonial Nigeria by the English Imperial Government and the Royal Niger Company was effected through Lugard overriding and eventually taking over the English Colonial structure in "Nigeria." In those years, up to 80% of the English Colonial expenditure on 'Nigeria' was reportedly for military purposes.

This only provided gasoline to fuel Lugard's quest for fame in his homeland though, and despite the colonial offices recommending various independent regions to reflect the complexity of Nigeria (not that they had the moral or legal right to), Lugard pushed for the most simple administrative setup and forced various countries into two protectorates to give him enough time (roughly about half of the year) to vacation in England, speaking at parties and social events about his African adventure.

This was to facilitate his desired climb up the English social ladder, which had been derailed by his moral indiscretions.

Acknowledgement

To God, the Father whose name is hallowed
The Almighty, All knowing Sovereign
Who subjects Himself to Righteousness and Justice
and as such to whom the means matter as much as the end

Dedication

To Wing Commander Chimda Stephen Hedima (October 1, 1977 - Circa October 1, 2014), captured as his aircraft came under fire, while providing cover to his at-risk and under fire Army comrades on the ground

and his copilot, Group Captain Abdulrasheed Bamidele Braimoh, still reported as Missing in Action as of 2021

To their comrades who have lost their lives, and to those maimed and injured in action

and to the thousands of Officers, Men and Women of the Nigerian Army, Navy and Air Force, swimming against the tidal wave of faulty foundations

Not asking questions, but serving, protecting, and preventing the innocent and defenseless from being completely overrun

Your predecessors chased the Italians out of Ethiopia and the horn of Africa, and the forgotten 81st and 82nd Divisions stalled the Japanese in Burma

ALSO

To millions who never got to know and love their homelands, due to the acts and crimes of slave raiders and traders

and to tens of millions who live deprived, unfulfilled, and ineffectual lives, due to the acts and crimes of soul traders

Table of Contents

References

The Fuduyan-Fulbe Takeover of Hausa Country

North Africa was a dangerous place for foreigners in the 18th century and the few centuries preceding it, as any student of American History and the Barbary Wars would recall. The kidnapping and enslavement campaign that reportedly entrapped hundreds of thousands of Europeans and pushed the United States into its first foreign war, also made North Africa a very dangerous route for intending Hajj pilgrims from the far Western Coast of Africa, including Futa (Fulbe, Fula) Toro and Futa Djallon.

Skirting the southern edges of the Sahara would have been a much safer, and in some ways, a more straightforward route to Arabia. It also brought these pilgrims, and other travelers and migrants, in contact with the indigenous countries of the Sahel, including the large Hausa country that is currently split between the post-colonial nations of Niger and Nigeria, which were created by the gathering convened by one of history's worst mass murderers and his European comrades, in what they labeled as the Berlin Conference.

Hausa country was prosperous, but fragmented, with frequent clashes and skirmishes between its constituent city-states. Kano was the largest city and commercial center, attracting merchants and caravans from across the Sahara in North Africa and other parts of the Mediterranean.

Despite the size and prominence of Kano, it was events in Gobir, a city-state to the northwest, which had a significant and lasting impact on Hausa country and the emergence of the Nigerian state.

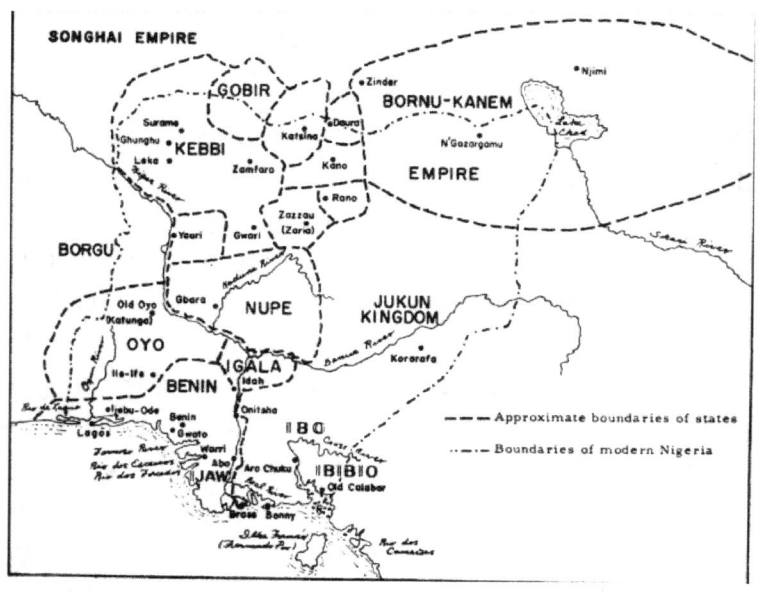

Map showing some the countries partly or wholly subjugated into the post-colonial Nigerian State [3]

Russian writer Lev (Leo) Tolstoy is credited with saying that "All great literature is one of two stories; A man goes on a journey, or a stranger comes to town." If this suggestion is true, then the history of the Berlin-mapped Nigerian State should make for some good reading, as two of the most central figures (Uthman Fuduye and Frederick Lugard) were strangers who rolled into town, with a desire for glory and the subjugation of the land and its peoples.

Both had good preparation.

Fuduye's mentor, Jubril Umar of Agadez, had been expelled from Gobir for starting extremist trouble. Umar had moved too soon, and his strategy did not have mass appeal (including the music and dancing) that Fuduye adopted as part of the initial strategy of gaining some popularity with the masses.

Fuduye was also extremely patient. Three decades passed and a few different Sarkins ruled Gobir, between Fuduye's arrival, and the ascension of Yunfa, Fuduye's former student, to the Gobir throne.

Gobir was on the Western edge of Hausa Country and was thus likely one of the first major city-states in Hausa Country that Fulbe pilgrims/migrants/tourists would encounter on their path to Sudan, and onwards to the Middle East.

Significantly, many indigenous Nigerian countries and cultures suggest that it is a virtue to be kind to 'strangers' and travelers. An Afeire saying even likens kindness to strangers with the proper upbringing of children (the most precious segment of society) with the saying that translates as 'Children are like strangers/travelers and it is duty of everyone to show them the right way' This duty and warmness towards 'strangers' has sadly also proven to be a vulnerability for which many indigenous Nigerian and African societies have paid a heavy price.

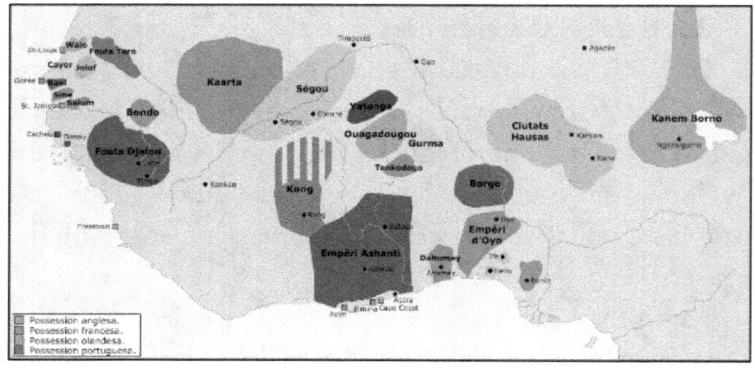

The distance between Hausa Country and Fulbe (Futa/ Fula) homelands of Futa Djalon and Futo Toro on Africa's far western tip is about 1500 miles (approx 2400 KM)

Fuduye's more patient, wider net strategy eventually led to the capitulation of Gobir, and within a few short years, with the reconnaissance and collaboration of allied and fellow Fulbe cattle-rearing militia/herdsmen, the overthrow of the Sarkins of Hausa Country.

The scale and speed with which Hausa country (Africa's wealthiest and one of the largest at the time) fell was astonishing and has sometimes been attributed some divine purpose and enablement. Fuduye was in Gobir for three decades before Gobir fell, but the Hausa city-states, and the entire country, fell like a set of dominoes within the next decade[4].

Some of the reasons for this rapid fall, which will be described below include i) Information and reconnaissance, ii) relative unity of purpose and iii) the fact that most people just want to get on with their lives and care little for politics and governance.

i. Information and reconnaissance:

The migrating (and some would say invading) Fulbe, are highly organized into structured clans and extended family groups. Some members of these clans began to transverse the Sahel belt that lies beneath the sahara desert with their cattle in the decades, or maybe centuries before Gobir's fall. These herdsmen, with superior knowledge of the countryside had sometimes been hired by the Hausa Sarkins in their quarrels against each other.

As such, while there were a few battles before Fuduye captured Gobir, it was relatively easy for the Fulbe clans to kill and take over the leadership of the other Hausa city-states and the rest of the country, as the herdsmen were already strategically located around the country and had some military responsibility (or past service) to the Sarkins in some places.

The impact of this cattle bearing militia extended beyond Hausa country, as herdsmen soon crossed the Niger (Kwara) River into Jebba, and got the consent of the Monarch in the region, the Alaafin (Abiodun), to graze cattle in the Country, on the condition that the cattle would not go into the villages and towns, or damage crops in farms.

A few decades later, a future Alaafin soon lost his War Camp, Ilorin, and his Capital Oyo to the foreign Fulbe clans, but unlike the Hausa Sarkins, the Monarchy survived, as the Alaafin moved 130 KM (80 miles) south, to Ago or Atiba, where the local Chief, the Ashipa, quickly stepped aside, to become a chief in the Alaafin's council, and allow the creation of an interim (later new) 'Oyo',

The stool of the Alaafin still sat at Atiba as at the passing of Alaafin Lamidi Adeyemi in 2022.

ii. Relative unity of purpose:

While the Hausa Sarkins were bickering and skirmishing, the Fulbe clans saw a rich and large country that was ripe for plucking, While the clanship structure and information advantages described above played an enabling role in the rapid takeover, the 'kill incentive', where the clan member who was quickest to turn the knife/sword on his host, and pledge allegiance to the Fuduyan Fulbe cause, became the new monarch of the city state he likely ventured into (or camped outside) a few years earlier, was key in motivating ambitious men in executing the cause.

This happened not just in the Hausa states, but in the adjoining Nupe country and in Ilorin, where Afonja, the Alaafin's general in charge of the garrison city, soon fell to the sword of Alimi, a Fulbe he had invited to the city. Others like Modibo Adama also executed the same strategy around Yola in the Northeast of the Nigerian state.

It was thus relatively easy for clan members to take thrones and territories from dispersed, disconnected and largely uninformed local monarchs.

iii. Indifference, powerlessness and ambivalence of the populace:

Most people just want to get on with their lives, and will adapt to a new regime or rulership, especially if public opposition to the new rule is met with the threat of severe sanctions and repercussions. Most realize that they are powerless to effectively oppose a new government or ruler, so they just accept their fate and hope for the best.

Think of an indigene or local resident of post-colonial Cameroon for instance. Following the criminal gathering in Berlin, his village and the surrounding areas are declared German territory, and he suddenly had to learn to speak German to transact any serious business or communication. The village and the surrounding areas are then tossed back and forth like a ball or hot potato between France, Germany and England over the next few decades as these European states jostle and scramble over territory that they had no right to. Sections of Cameroon were sometimes used as chips and extras in other transactions and negotiations, including bargaining for other 'colonies' like Morocco.

Following a series of actions, skirmishes and settlements between these Europeans (including the Agadir crisis, the treaty of Fez, and the 'World Wars', various parts German Kamerun and Neukamerun were incorporated into parts of the post-colonial nations of Chad, Congo, Gabon, Central African Republic, Nigeria, and as at 2023, the separatist region and possible future nation of Ambazonia.

Depending on events, transactions and negotiations happen very far away from him, and that are certainly not to his benefit, the post-colonial Cameroonian is tossed back and forth, sliced and diced into and between nations conjured from warmongering and profit-seeking European minds. These crimes and actions, like several before them, immediately get the seal of approval of the League of Nations, or whatever international entity that exists to protect and validate the decisions and interests of its controlling and founding members.

So, our Cameroonian, who just wants to live a peaceful and productive life, goes from speaking his own language, to officially speaking German, English and French in a few short decades.

These issues are not just memories of a distant colonial past, but remain very real in in 2024, where English speaking Ambazonia, which has been the victim of some of the most criminal and egregious international decisions, is pummeled to remain part of a French speaking Cameroon, led by a 91 year old Paul Biya, with French support as part of its Francafrique philosophy.

Moving back to Nigeria and Hausa Country, George Douglas Hazzeldine, writing in 1904 with limited information and from jaundiced perspective of documenting just how much of a steal England's grab of (most of) the Fulbe ruled Hausa was, penned his thoughts on the remarkable and relatively swift takeover of Hausa County by the Fulbe clans as follows:

Othman was a Fulani, who, having for some time provided petty kings with the sinews of war, conceived the advantages of fighting for himself and of getting the profits of the principal as well as the commission of the agent. We have only a general outline of his career, but it probably began with wealth, and it certainly ended in power. The Hausa kings, jealous of one another, went down one by one before this unexpected conqueror, and bowed their heads to the power they had turned against one another so often in the past.

Othman succeeded beyond all possible dreams. It was a mighty life-work, to come into the world a member of a homeless race[5], a lender of money, a mercenary fighter of other men's quarrels, and to leave it the temporal and the spiritual head, the arbitrary master, of a consolidated people, the lord of an empire rivaling that of the Moor at its best. The Moor, conquering half Spain and almost reaching Egypt, ruled a greater territory but fewer people than did the Sultan of Sokoto, whose word was law to millions, and whose power extended from Lake Chad almost to the lakes of the Upper Niger, from the sands of the desert almost to the sands of the sea.

Having conquered, this dark Napoleon, like the white one, set himself to administer. Among his own race, he found his material. Everywhere he appointed governors and petty governors of his own people. The officials, military, civil, fiscal and judicial, from the highest to the lowest, all were Fulani. The original Hausa made no objection. Just as the Fulani had dwelt with him before, tending the cattle of the country, living beside him but keeping to himself, so the Fulani continued, carrying on the administration and protection of the country.

This is not to suggest that all of Hausa country fell in line with the Fuduyan Fulbe takeover, but the structure of the country as City-States meant that the death of a few key monarchs and the takeover of the key cities made others align and surrender, with religion and tribute as the key markers and condition of this alignment. As such, religion was both a tool of control, and proof of submission.

Those who failed to align, migrated to surrounding countries, and only a few short decades later, a significant number of the Alaafin of Oyo's horsemen were ethnic Hausa for instance. A few more decades down the line, some of their descendants formed a ready pool for recruitment into Lugard's West African Frontier Force, and its earlier iterations.

Others moved into the deep hinterland of Hausa Country, far from the capital cities and major areas of the city-states. away from the interest and direct influence of their new conquerors. Members of this group were essentially stripped of their Hausa identity and became (or were lumped with the pre-existing group already) known as Maguzawa.

The Treaty of Tordesillas and European Scramble

Have you ever wondered why Portuguese is spoken in Brazil, while Spanish is spoken in most of the rest of South and Latin America? Or why the Portuguese visit Bini (Edo), Angola, Fernando Po (Bioko) and other parts of Africa ahead of other Europeans in the 15th century?

In 1494, following the visit of Columbus to America, and other expeditions around the time, Spain and Portugal, the two nations of the Iberian Peninsula decided that there was enough of the non-European world for conquest and there was no need to squabble or fight each other doing so.

The treaty of Tordesillas divided the world into two, via a straight line, with the demarcation line about halfway between Cape Verde (claimed by Portugal) and Cuba (claimed by Spain). The Spanish born Pope Alexander (born Rodrigo Borgia) happily ratified this agreement.

A few centuries later, driven by even more greed and criminal intentions, representatives of more European nations gathered in Berlin for some more division and map drawing. Their range had narrowed from the entire world to the African continent, and the demarcation lines this time were not straight, and often made no sense, as plundering of resources took priority over the existing national and cultural realities on ground.

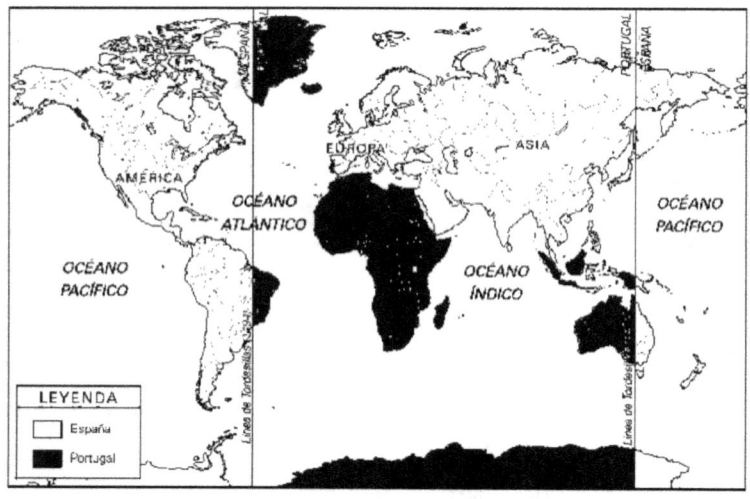

The world according to the treaty of Tordesillas

The time in between Tordesillas and Berlin should aptly be described as Europe unleashing chaos on the world. Other European nations, who were developing navigational and maritime capacity, soon got in on the act, and with the 'no honor among thieves' mode, and the 'might is right' mindset, refused to recognize the Spanish and Portuguese agreement.

England, France and Holland were particularly aggressive in establishing 'colonies' in Africa, the Americas, Asia, and the Caribbean.

There was no consideration for the indigenous peoples of these lands in the plundering madness of these Nations and their rulers. Terrorists and plunderers like Francis Drake were knighted and celebrated by their home nations.

From Tordesillas to Berlin

While there were almost four centuries from Tordesillas till the Berlin rendezvous, only about 10% of the African continent was under the control of Europeans by 1870, the decade before the criminal gathering that was labeled and whitewashed as a conference.

In the four to five decades between Berlin and Europe's first world war, about 90% of the African continent had come under European control.

It is extremely important to note that the plundering of the continent was in full effect, even before colonization was 'formalized' in Berlin. The Berlin gathering was arranged mostly for the purpose of avoiding conflict by putting some order (from the European perspective) to the ongoing plundering.

Unlike the Americas where there was a massive influx of 'conquistadors' and settlers from Europe, Sub-Saharan Africa did not experience a massive wave of European immigrants outside of the Southern tip of the continent, especially the post-colonial nations of Republic of South Africa and Zimbabwe. Angola also had a few hundred thousand Portuguese.

It is certainly much easier to exert and maintain control with a resident military force and administrative machinery, but West Africa had an unexpected ally that curtailed large scale European immigration for a few centuries after Tordesillas: Malaria and the Anopheles Mosquito.

We'll get back to Malaria and the Mosquito in a bit.

The Atlantic Meets the Sahara

The inability to physically occupy Sub-Saharan (especially West) Africa on a widespread basis was no barrier or limit to the plundering of the continent however, as it became the intersection and a crosspoint of two of the most horrific and aggressive slave campaigns in history, the trans-Atlantic and trans-Saharan slave campaigns.

The Fuduyan Fulbes who gained control of Hausa country (rightly or wrongly) used a religious justification for their war and slave campaigns, though there was little hesitation in declaring war and raiding existing Islamic states and communities, as their drawn-out war with Kanem-Bornu, Hausa Country's Northeastern neighbor, shows.

It should be noted that the post-colonial Bornu that is within the Nigerian State is only the Southern tip of the Kanem-Bornu Empire, which in the past ran all the way from Libya in North Africa, through most of post-colonial Chad and Eastern boundaries of Niger. This territory was a critical part of the trans-Saharan trade (and slave) route and connected to Tripoli (reportedly the largest slave market in the mediterranean) through Agadez and Bilma in post-colonial Niger.

It is very likely that the control of the slave routes and markets were a factor in the war between the Kanuris (as indigenes of Kanem are known) and the Fuduyan Fulbes.

Kanem was however much better prepared than Hausa country, as its location in what has historically been an unstable and war-prone corridor made it experienced with dealing with and reacting to invasions. The kingdom had moved its capital at different points in reaction to attempted invasions and annexations. Kukawa, Dikwa, Gazargamu (Birin Gazaramu) are Kanem capitals that fell to invasion and takeover attempts by the Fuduyan Fulbes, the French, and the Sudanese warlord Rabih Az Zubayr. In each case, the loss of the capital did not result in a successful and sustained takeover of the kingdom[6]. In more recent times, the current seat of the Shehu of Borno, Maiduguri and the surrounding areas have been under pressure from Boko Haram.

Rabih's problems with the French arose partly because he was very eager to reach an agreement with the English and cede the land and kingdom to English colonialism in the emerging post-Berlin chaos. The English probably viewed Az-Zubayr as a very recent usurper, with a shaky hold on power and felt the Fuduyan Fulbes, also foreign but with a much longer hold on power, represented a much firmer and efficient route to control of large portions of its Berlin-drawn territories. The subjugation and retention of Fuduyan control over most of Hausa country would have to happen first, and a certain Frederick Lugard was the man hired for that task.

It is therefore not surprising that Az-Zubayr was engaged in battles with the Fuduyan Fulbe's, before French ambitions demanded his attention, and eventually, his life.

It is tragic, that foreign groups and peoples, Europeans and people identifying as Arabic, were the key planners, drivers, and operators of the Saharan and Atlantic slave trade in many of the countries that constitute the Nigerian state.

About a century before Az-Zubayr, Fuduye's son and successor, Mohammed Bello, led brutal campaigns and raids to consolidate power, crush dissent, and invariably, capture slaves.

Among the dissenters crushed was Hausa leader Abd al-Salam Ibrahim, whose alleged oppression and persecution by the Sarkin (Monarch of) Gobir, was used as a major reason for the Fuduyan uprising. Abd al-Salam's key role in the uprising lent its credibility as a religious and not a foreign ethnic takeover.

He soon however learned the bitter lesson (as would a certain Afonja in Ilorin decades later) that working with outsiders for a foreign takeover of your own country usually ends in personal tragedy, despite the initial gain it may promise. Feeling dissatisfied with the rewards and the position he got upon the Fuduyan takeover of the country; he began to attract and lead similarly dissatisfied Hausa regime changers but was killed in a raid of his settlement in Kware by Mohammed Bello's forces.

Gaining control of Hausa country did not translate to running it successfully though as the Fuduyan Fulbe rulers were unable to maintain the norms and balance that made Hausa country the wealthiest in Africa before Fuduye rolled into town. Mohammed Bello, Fuduye's son and successor, settled for the 'low hanging fruit' of a slave raiding economy, within a few decades, there were over two million slaves in Hausa Country, second only to the Southern United States in terms of slaves for any country in the world at the time.

Most of the victims of these crimes were traded to the Arab world through the trans-Saharan route, but as the account of Crowther and other victims have shown, the Fuduyan Fulbes had direct contact with Portuguese and other European slave traders. The repeated wars and raid attempts by the Fuduyan Fulbes on Oyo (in Post-colonial Nigeria's southwest) and Borno (in Post Colonial Nigeria's Northeast may thus be explained as economically motivated, even if given a religious spin or cover.

The commission for the Southern charge toward the Atlantic Ocean on 'Nigeria's' Eastern flank was given to Fuduye allied Fulbe clan leader Modibbo Adama, but not much progress was made on that front as the indigenous ethnic nations in what is post-colonial Nigeria's middle belt resisted the invasions and slave raiding attempts with some success.

Accounts by the Tiv, a middle-belt ethnic nationality, claim that Fuduye himself was wounded in one of the attempts to invade their country, but these claims have been disputed by the Fuduyan-Fulbes.

As Jihadist invaders consolidated their hold on Nigeria's largest country and made incursions southward, Western Europe's charge on Africa, and the rest of the world, entered a frenzied and renewed phase.

The flame first ignited at Tordesillas four centuries earlier, was now a raging inferno consuming the entire continent, and the host of the firestorm convened to plunder the continent and was none other than the mass murderer of millions of Africans. The Belgian Monarch, Leopold.

It seemed there was some sort of cosmic joke on Africans suggesting that if Mohammed Bello, the resident jihadist invader from 1500 miles away could slaughter thousands and enslave over two million, then Leopold, the non-resident European invader could up the ante and slaughter up to 10 million. More Africans were killed by Leopold than Jews by Hitler.

Yet, the countries of Western Europe had no qualms gathering around the table of the mass murderer to share loot and plunder and create a new world (or African) order, which is completely anti-African in design and outcomes in many ways. Sadly, this still defines the global context within which Africans, with their Berlin created countries, are forced to operate.

The surge that prompted Leopold's criminal gathering takes us back to Malaria, the mosquito, and their surprising but extremely important impact on colonialism.

In the centuries following Tordesillas, other countries in Western Europe saw Spain and Portugal create wealth from the returns of their partitioning of the world. These countries quickly joined the plundering and refused to recognize the partitioning agreement by Spain and Portugal.

In a clear case of there being no honor amongst thieves, it became a case of 'hold it to prove that you own it', and while this proved to be a problem for Portugal in Africa, it was an opportunity for countries like Germany, France, England, Netherlands and the Franco-Dutch alloy nation of Belgium to get a slice of the continent.

'Holding it' sometimes involved the mass murder of hundreds of thousands or millions of indigenous people to subdue and control the land or country. While the horrors of these actions are generally understated and underreported for Africa, the case of Belgium's Leopold in Congo is a reminder of the sheer scale and terror that Europe unleashed in the world.

The indigenous countries of Nigeria were not spared from the scorched Earth policy that usually served as a precursor to gain control and establish the 'hold it to own it' principle. Beginning with the bombardment of Lagos in 1851, and further unprovoked, or deliberately instigated military confrontations in Ijebu and Benin City, England used the destruction of these regional capital cities to signal that it had the 'biggest guns' and it was willing to slaughter at will to show that it was the new sheriff in town, at least as far as indigenous countries and communities were concerned, and it could only be rivaled by the big guns of its competing European plunderers.

An Effort to Partner and not Plunder

Even as Europe made a late charge to grab whatever piece of Africa it could in the 19th century, there were efforts that recognized the inherent evil of the path that was taken, and tried to suggest and even implement a different approach, where Africans could participate in what was rapidly changing world on a somewhat equal footing. An approach where Africans could speak for themselves and defend their resources and land in a world where might was right, regardless of the evil perpetrated by that might.

One of the more notable efforts in this regard involved Ajayi Crowther and the ill-fated and oddly named Colonial or Niger expedition of 1841, 10 years before England began its charge into what is now Nigeria with the bombardment of Lagos in 1851.

The general idea behind this expedition was that Africans could springboard into an equal footing in the new world with trade, education and religion (or the three Cs of commerce, Christianity and civilization as they put it). The promoters of the Expedition hoped that making treaties with a few key kingdoms and countries would be an alternative to slavery and colonialism, enabling Africans to make progress and work for their own best interests in the emerging world.

This expedition, no matter how well intentioned, had two critical flaws. The first flaw was ignoring or not accounting for the grim reality of the world back then (and largely since) that might be essentially translated as right, and there was no contingency for this. Perhaps the plan was to ensure that these countries and nationalities became vassals, with England enjoying privileged commercial rights and providing military protection and weaponry that will be paid for by the vassal states.

The second limitation or threat that scuttled this effort was the anopheles mosquito, even though no one knew this at the time. All that was known was that the forest region of West Africa beyond the coast had proven to be highly mortal for Europeans, so much so that the region was referred to as the white man's graveyard.

At the time, it was assumed that the air was just unsuitable for European lungs, hence the name malaria which translates to 'bad air.' The good and noble intentions of the voyagers of the Niger Expedition did not spare them from the devastating effects of the 'bad air' of West Africa. Of the 159 Europeans who were part of the expedition, 55 died within a few months, a fatality rate of almost 40%. At least 130 of the Europeans fell ill during the expedition, before it was called off.

This expedition's casualty rate, as devastating as it was, was 'better' than previous attempts by England to physically occupy West Africa with its military. Between 1817 and 1837, the attempts of the English to militarily occupy West Africa for any extended periods led to a mortality rate of about 50% among the troops for what was assumed to be the Bad-Air or Mal-Aria. [7]

It was obvious that military bombardments or a scorched earth policy would be a much more efficient and effective approach for England to achieve its objectives for the countries and ethnic nationalities that were eventually bundled into the Nigerian state.

The fall of Oyo, the abundance of thousands of Hausa men fleeing the chokehold of the Fuduyan Fulbes in their country made the environment just right for English intentions. There was no Central military Authority to coordinate a widespread resistance to English incursions, and there were a lot of potential fighting men who could be recruited to provide the non-commissioned support for an invading, and later on, an occupying Army.

Lagos, Ijebu and Benin were ripe for bombardments and attacks from the coast, and a couple of quick and destructive raids on these key cities made everyone else fall in line and accede to England as the dominant power and influence. However, Malaria was still the major obstacle for the English (and other Europeans) to establish and maintain a physical presence as the governing authority.

It would take the cleaning up of the Mal-Aria (Bad-Air) that was killing many Europeans that ventured beyond the coast of West Africa to the interior, for that physical governing presence to be established.

Cleaning Up the Air

There was and is no problem with the African air, of course, and Malaria caused havoc among indigenous communities as well. The big difference was that most of the African fatalities from malaria were young children and the devastation and high infant mortality caused by the disease led to the 'Ogbanje' or 'Abiku' myth in some indigenous Nigerian societies.

This also meant that the surviving population of youth and adults developed a relative resistance to malaria due to long term exposure to the malaria antigens[8]

The 'bad air' was however getting in the way of big ambitions and business, and the colonial offices of England, France and other European countries poured resources into finding a solution. It was only a matter of time before the 'protection' from direct occupation that Malaria provided would crumble.

The breakthrough came as Patrick Manson was able to show the association between insects, specifically mosquitoes, and pathogens causing human and animal diseases. It was no surprise that this occurred during his employment with the Colonial Office in China around 1868.

The European Colonial offices, and the private profiteers from slavery and colonialism continued to pour resources into Malaria research, and it was no surprise that the first two schools of tropical Medicine were in Liverpool and London, two of the largest slave trading ports (along with Bristol) in England.[9]

The progress in medicine only took European crimes and the plundering scramble for Africa to a frenzied pace and it was only when these criminal activities were about to spill over into European nations fighting wars against each other the plunder from Africa that Leopold, perhaps the biggest criminal of all, decided to convene a conference in Berlin, to be hosted by the German Chancellor, Otto Van Bismark in 1884.

Sandwiching Leopold's Berlin Conference was another significant discovery in the deconstruction of malaria.

Alphonse Laveran, a French Colonial doctor working in Algeria, identified the causal agent (or plasmodium) of malaria in 1880. Further progress was made in 1890, as Ronald Ross, a British colonial officer working in India demonstrated that the mosquito was responsible for the transmission of malaria.

The leaders in the field of tropical medicine, the Liverpool and London schools of Tropical Medicine, and their French (*Société de Pathologie Exotique*) and Portuguese counterparts, were primarily set up to 'facilitate colonial expansion'[10].

Laveran and Ross deservedly later won Nobel prizes for their work, but more significantly, with the progress made with malaria research, the pathway to full colonialism was now clear and the likes of Lugard and other adventurists could lead the charge with a large deployment of troops now able to spend considerable time further inland. The whole attack playbook was now open, as opposed to the previous limited options of coastal bombardments, and short inland raids of key cities and capitals close to the coast.

Correcting False Narratives

It is extremely important to address and put some balance to growing and seemingly well-orchestrated campaigns and narratives that attempt to whitewash the horrors of slavery and other crimes of subjugation. These narratives also water down the malicious intent of the organizers and profiteers of these crimes, whose successors and descendants, while not being responsible for these crimes, are direct beneficiaries of it.

In many cases, the sovereign nations, institutions, parliaments and royal houses that were the perpetrators of these crimes are still 'going concerns' and continuing entities. The English Parliament and Belgian Monarchy are clear cases in point.

1. The first major narrative to be considered, especially for the transatlantic slave trade is the suggestion that the development of the 'modern' corporation, and not European Governments or Royal Houses, is to be blamed. It proposes that the corporation made it possible for hundreds and possibly thousands of people who did not know each other, to pull capital for a common goal and objective. This common goal and objective were to seek the best investment and economic opportunities and get the best return on capital, which at that time turned out to be new territories, and getting slaves from sub-Saharan Africa to power the agriculture of these new territories. As such it is really nobody's fault since the capital

raised for long defunct companies like the Dutch East India Company and the Royal Niger company was responsible for these horrific crimes.

2. The next major narrative gaining traction is that Sub-Saharan Africans were already significantly involved in massive slave trades and Arabs and Europeans simply latched on and played very minor roles in the capturing and trafficking of Africans whose brethren and communities lifted no finger in their defense and offered no resistance to these invasions or the slave trade.

It should be already obvious that the first set of narratives are inconsistent and generally not mutually or logically compatible. If the rise of the modern corporation made it possible to raise large amounts of capital which enabled the mobilization of weapons, ships and other resources needed to pursue profit, and we certainly know that sub-Saharan Africans were neither contributors to nor managers of this capital, then suggesting that Africans were just as responsible for the slave trade is clearly untrue and outrightly ridiculous..

3. The third growing narrative is that the victims and perpetrators of these horrendous crimes are long gone, and discussions of these events are unnecessarily divisive as it is too late to have any form of accountability by the perpetrators or provide any comfort or justice to the victims.

4. A fourth narrative, which is usually implied, but is an especially effective approach to quash and hide the hideous crimes of slavery usually revolves around threats, suggesting that attempts to recount or examine what are extremely ungodly and shameful acts, amount to the desecration of some holy or religious figure or text that will not be tolerated in any

form, and could be met with severely punitive and even violent repercussions.

We will address each of these narratives that try to obscure or outrightly falsify the truth, below.

We already know that the first two narratives are logically inconsistent, since the well-funded and focused corporations with their ships and armed muscle were going to get African slaves as labor for new territories, regardless of the so-called pre-existing cultural practices that are now claimed as a defense or justification.

Corporations and not Nations?

However, the attempts to delink sovereign European nations like France, England, Germany and Portugal, or the Belgian Monarchy from slavery and colonialism, and shift the blame to defunct corporations is an exercise in falsehood and futility.

European nations, represented by their leadership, including their monarchs, royal houses, governments and legislatures were active promoters, drivers and enforcers of slavery and colonialism, and often deployed their military might and resources to promote and defend the rights and interests of these corporations, when not acting directly.

In the case of Nigeria, the English Parliament paid its Royal Niger Company[11] for the 'ownership' of the 'protectorates' that had been criminally cobbled together from previously independent, self-sustaining and unaffiliated countries.

These countries, parliaments and royal houses are clearly liable for these criminal acts, and while they may never be held accountable, the attempts to falsify and whitewash history should not go unchallenged.

Minor Roles in Crimes on Non-Resisting Victims

The suggestion that Arabs and Europeans merely tethered and latched on to massive ongoing slave trade by Africans who offered no resistance to these external parties is also false and ridiculous. The ships and caravans were not invited or organized by Africans, and origins of whatever religious texts there were used to rightly or wrongly initiate and justify these crimes were certainly not African.

The narrative that Africans were willing participants or victims who offered no organized resistance to the slave raids and trade is also untrue as shown by the examples of Kanem-Bornu and Oyo, two of the larger countries that were pulled into the colonies or 'protectorates' that were eventually configured by the English as Nigeria.

Bornu mostly sits on Nigeria's northeastern corner, while Oyo was a leading sub-ethnicity of the Afeire confederation that mostly lies in Nigeria's southwestern corner.

There are accounts of the rulers of Bornu (Mai and later Shehu) writing to the leaders of Arab states in North Africa, demanding an end to slave raids in their territories and wondering why these raids were carried out on fellow Moslem countries. The resistance of Bornu to Arab slave raids were not limited to cease and desist letters. Villages and communities took action to safeguard their populace, similar to those in Oyo and surrounding areas.

From Hugh Clapperton's account of his journey through Bornu:

More dangerous were the traps constructed by villagers on Borno's borders to prevent Tuareg incursions into their country – 'some of them were about 12 feet deep, square at the top and tapering at the bottom having 4 pointed sticks sticking up at the bottom – the top is covered with a little grass and reeds over which is strewed sand so that they look like the best sand - they are about 4 or 5 feet wide at the top[12].

Moving down to Oyo, which was not an empire in the true sense of the word, but the most militant sub-ethnicity that viewed itself as the defender and security leader of the confederation, we see a similar pattern of a strong resistance to external slave raiding by the 'government' or leadership, and self-help efforts by communities to resist slave raiding, after the fall of Oyo.

Oyo's location on the northern frontier of the confederation gave it a natural security role where it historically had moments of skirmishes and longer periods of friendly relations with the neighboring countries (Nupe and Borgu) on this frontier. The confederation was bordered on the South by the Atlantic Ocean, on the East by the culturally linked (by leadership) Bini or Edo Kingdom, and to the Northeast by the even more culturally related Igala ethnic group.

As such the northern front was the primary area of concern, and this made Afonja's rebellion and the subsequent fall of Ilorin tragic for Oyo and the confederation. Before then, the Afeire confederacy had been shielded from both the trans-Atlantic and the trans-Saharan slave trades by Oyo's securing role. Oyo's rulers tried to promote the spirit of the confederacy by mostly appointing non-natives of Oyo as the head of its Army (Aare Ona Kakanfo), but conflict was not uncommon due to issues relating to cultural hierarchies and tributes Oyo felt it deserved and demanded, since it was on the hostile 'frontline', and the other 'sub-nationals' enjoyed the benefits and relative peace from its securing role.

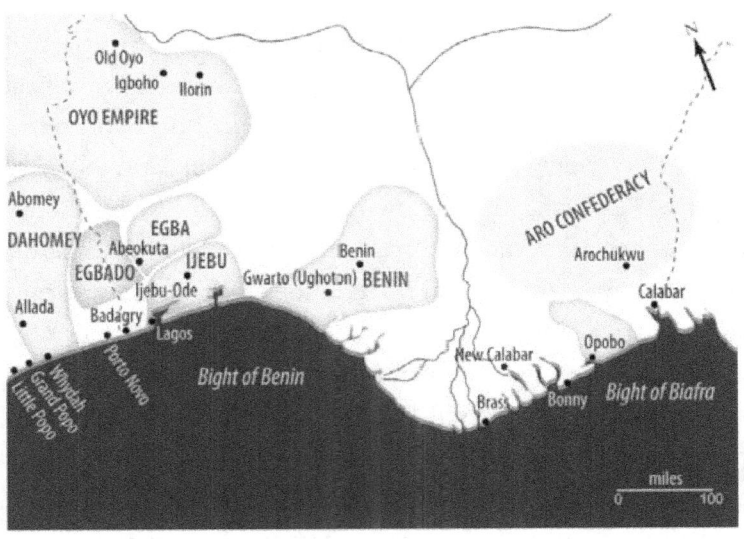

Source: https://i0.wp.com/thinkafrica.net/wp-content/uploads/2020/06/word-image-5.png?resize=1024%2C741&ssl=1

Eventually, Ilorin, and then Oyo fell to the foreign Fulbe jihadists, and the effects on Afeire confederacy was '*catastrophic as they had largely avoided being made slaves up to that point but were now by far the majority of those captured and shipped to the Americas until the slave trade ended here in the 1850s*'[13]

It is not surprising that despite Oyo's resistance to both the Arab and European slave trades (or at least its attempt to protect its confederate nation from both), western accounts often tries to force the narrative of a slave trading Oyo, with one such account stating that *'Despite an oral tradition that minimizes the Oyo's involvement in the slave trade, the Oyo Empire certainly used slaves within its own state structures - many officials in the administration and military, for example, were of slave origin, much more so than in other states in the region.'*

The reality is that oral traditions have no sensitivities to modern feelings towards slavery and no reason to try to appeal to such sensitivities. While disputes over tributes and traditional hierarchies led to military action and war captives, these captives were still in their own country and were not condemned to a lifetime of forced servitude and unpaid labor, and even by western written accounts, many of the war captives rose to become leading military and civilian officials.

We also see a similar pattern to the case in Borno, where smaller villages put up self-help defense efforts to resist external slave raiders, based on the account of the well-known precolonial era 'Nigerian,' Samuel Ajayi Crowther.

Before recounting Crowther's ordeal, it is worth mentioning that in addition to the breakdown of the state and security structure, the fall of Oyo led to a massive refugee crisis where hundreds of thousand, and possibly up to a million people wandered southwards with no real destination, but away from the known danger.

Outside of Oyo, the Afeire confederacy had nothing close to a central government or security force, and the cultural reverence for Ile-Ife had no military or political significance. The 12-15 'Confederate states' were mostly structured in a similar fashion, with a central town, king and market, surrounded by hundreds of smaller towns, villages and farming communities.

It was in one of these smaller towns surrounding Oyo, that Ajayi Crowther was born.

As such, there was no basis or platform for a coordinated response to this massive refugee crisis, even though some of the monarchs helped with the formation of new towns for the refugees in the borders of their territories. Modakeke, on the border of Ile-Ife territory and Osogbo on the border of Ijesha territory are examples of new towns created for refugees from this crisis. Ibadan is probably the most famous new city that emerged from the crisis, though its development was not linked to the actions or response of a Monarch to the crisis.

Despite the 'development' of these new towns, there were likely hundreds of thousands of refugees roaming the country, and the conditions for slave raiding and trading were set following the fall of Oyo, with raiders from the North, Portuguese and other European slave ships on the coast, and no central security force. A number of rogue domestic slave traders undoubtedly got in on the act, including the relatively well-known Madam Tinubu.

These conditions are what took Afeire confederacy indigenes[14] from almost being completely insulated from the Atlantic slave trade to become probably the worst victims of the trade in some decades of the 19th century.

Coming back to Crowther, his first-hand account of the slave raid that captured him and destroyed his town provides a candid camera of the operations of the Fuduyan Fulbe slave-based economy, and its dealings with European (Portuguese in this case) slave merchants. It also shows the defense put up by villages and smaller towns (wooden fences, guards and sentries, and the four-hour resistance to the surprise attack from a large slave raiding army).

Ajayi's account (partly excerpted below) deals another blow to the growing false narrative regarding the role of indigenous Africans in the slave trade.

The morning in which my town, Ocho-gu (Osogun), shared the same fate which many others had experienced, was fair and delightful; and most of the inhabitants were engaged in their respective occupations. We were preparing breakfast without any apprehension; when, about 9 o'clock a.m. a rumor was spread in the town that the enemies had approached with intentions of hostility. It was not long after when they had almost surrounded the town, to prevent any escape of the inhabitants; the town being rudely fortified with a wooded fence, about four miles in circumference, containing about 12,000 inhabitants, which would produce 3,000 fighting men. The inhabitants not being duly prepared, some not being at home; those who were, having about six gates to defend, as well as many weak places about the fence to guard against, and, to say in a few words, the men being surprised, and therefore confounded – the enemies entered the town after about three or four hours' resistance.[15]

Let Sleeping Dogs Lie

It is true that Leopold of Belgium is dead, as are the members of the English parliament that authorized the payment of Nigeria's purchase from the Royal Niger Company. However, the Belgian monarchy still exists and Leopold's descendants and associated institutions are beneficiaries of his crimes.

The effects of the plundering by the likes of Leopold and other Colonials, as devastating as it was, however pales in comparison to the damage done by the structural and statutory changes imposed on Africans by outsiders whose primary aim was to loot and plunder. The institutions and systems created by these crimes have become severe restrictions and limitations to the development of many African societies and need to be untangled.

It is important to note that no society can develop without significant investment in human capital, which would usually lead to capital formation and as such calls for reparations cannot and should not be a priority ahead of fixing the legal and fiscal mess that the criminal events in Berlin implanted these 'Nations', by their very creation.

Don't Touch or Harm the Anointed Prophets

While the Atlantic slave trade has attempted to blame commerce and the corporation for its rise, the Saharan slave trade does not hide its religious reasoning and motivation. Those who were not of the same religion were allowed to be enslaved and trafficked, under the right, and somewhat broad, conditions.

So, while a case may be made that sub-Saharan Africans were not more susceptible to slave raids from a racial standpoint, this case is immediately weakened by the fact that perpetrators and participants in these crimes justified their acts and decisions with texts from which inferences that maligned Africans (including likening Satan to black Africans) were rightly or wrongly made.

The trans-Saharan trade may yet pull up the commercial defense as well, especially since significant raids continued against black Muslims in Borno, and there were cases of European slaves held for ransom in North Africa. The Fuduyan-Fulbe rulers of Hausa Country may be the best case for a 'commercial' defense, as they turned war and slave campaigns into a sustainability and economic tool, rivaling the American South in leading the world in the number of captive slaves, as the economy of the previously wealthy Hausa country declined.

Religious justification for the Atlantic and Saharan slave trades ranged from the so-called curse on Ham and Canaan, to texts suggesting that the offspring created by God from Adam's left shoulder were as Black as Charcoal and destined for hell.

While it may be argued that these texts are metaphorical and open to interpretation, there is no doubt that they, and other writings by leading religious figures and stalwarts, were used as motivation or justification for crimes against millions of black Africans. There is also no argument or equivocacy about the mindset that produces texts and writings that state the following:

blacks as "people who are by their very nature slaves."

"All African women are prostitutes, and the whole race of African men are abeed (slave) stock."

black people are like "rats plaguing the earth."

"merriment dominates the black man because of his defective brain, whence also the weakness of his intelligence."

"If (all types of men) are taken, from the first, and one placed after another, like the Negro from Zanzibar, in the

Southern-most countries, the Negro does not differ from an animal in anything except the fact that his hands have been lifted from the earth -in no other peculiarity or property – except for what God wished. Many have seen that the ape is more capable of being trained than the Negro, and more intelligent."

"[The Zanj (African) differ from animals only in that] their two hands are lifted above the ground, ... Many have observed that the ape is more teachable and more intelligent than the Zanj."

"Therefore, the Negro nation are, as a rule, submissive to slavery, because [Negroes] have little [that is essentially] human and have attributes that are quite similar to those of dumb animals, as we have stated."

"beyond [known peoples of black West Africa] to the south there is no civilization in the proper sense. There are only humans who are closer to dumb animals than to rational beings. They live in thickets and caves, and eat herbs and unprepared grain. They frequently eat each other. They cannot be considered human beings."

These statements, credited to intellectuals who are also proudly promoted as titans in religious thinking and ideology, without doubt inspired and provided justification for centuries of slave raiding and genocide against black Africans.

It is almost certain that none of these brainiacs[16] had been south of the Sahara, or lived in a black African society, and their interaction or observation of Africans was likely limited to traumatized[17] and enslaved Africans who had been captured and trafficked across the Sahara and then likely castrated by their captors. Captured women were often forced into sex slavery, hence the soulless quote about African women, credited to Ibn Sina (Avi Cenna).

Thankfully, and somewhat hilariously, the seemingly crazed obsession to feel superior to the black African almost always self-propels into a brick wall with pseudo-scientific religious suggestions of the sub-humanity of the black African totally shattered by other studies and findings that the black African might actually be the purest homo-sapiens. Expectedly, this inconvenient suggestion is countered by other suggestions of ghost DNA that may make up to 20% West Africans.

What is certainly not funny or hilarious is to see a young girl in Ikeja, Lagos Nigeria dropped off by her mother in a school that commands one of the highest fees in the city, and is curiously named after the brainiac that had the most unpleasant thing to say about African women.

Fela Kuti would have had a field day with that one. Maybe he did, with Colomentality and Movement Against Second Slavery.

While it may seem unfair to judge brilliant men and women with significant intellectual achievements solely on the basis of their bias against black Africans, their baseless and hateful comments should not be excused or overlooked as well, regardless of the esteem in which their own stock, or the rest of the world holds them.

David, who penned the oft quoted Psalm about not harming prophets, was not giving a directive, but was telling how God protected Abraham and Isaac from unfriendly Kings during their travels. David himself, who was described as a man after God's heart, was severely cautioned, when his wandering eyes led him into Adultery.

Creating Nigeria

Lugard had fine-tuned his glory seeking skills as a sanctioned, but unofficial Muscle/Mercenary for English interests in Bugandaland, following his disgraceful exit from the British Army. The opportunity of raising a force in 'Nigeria' he could control outside of the official colonial channels, but with the presumed backing of the English Crown was too good to pass up.

Fuduye believed or prophesied that his (clan's) adventure in Hausa Country would last for 100 years, and would be ended by another foreigner, so he gave instructions for onward movement to the banks of the Nile in the Sudan.

Lugard, with a militia (Glover's Hausas) answerable to him, sidestepped his 'Mission to Borgu,' and faced Hausaland's slave raiding Fulbe clan leaders, somewhat fulfilling Fuduye's prediction, but then reinstalled the clan leaders on the condition of allegiance to the English crown.

Lugard then left for Hong Kong, and returned (for half the year, most of the time) to create the framework and amalgamation for what is by and large the post-colonial Nigerian State.

While the motive and strategy for the creation of the Nigerian State lies in the plundering and colonial interests of Europe and its interplay with the Fuduyan Jihadist control of Hausa Country, the tool and means of establishing that control was the 'Nigerian' Military.

It can be argued that the Nigerian Military has been the most significant force and factor, in the history, politics, and indeed the very existence of the Nigerian Nation, since Flora Shaw coined the name 'Nigeria' in 1897, and in the few decades before that moment. Shaw's naming move helped distinguish the 'French owned' Upper Niger areas (Niger), from the 'English owned' Lower Niger areas, with the Hausa country split almost down the middle between the two 'European owned' territories.

The impact of the Military on Nigerian existence has been so deep and wide, that a cursory reference on its sometimes unifying and/or defining role, will be grossly inefficient, as significantly more time and words will have to be expended to cogently capture and communicate this impact. This might be a blessing for the millions of Nigerians who passed through school with no relevant and contemporary History as part of the curriculum[18], in what can only be described as an attempt to suppress the truth. This will however still be a summarized version of a subject area that is begging for much more research, documentation, presentation to the public and for posterity.

Men of the military have been used (and have sometimes acted on their own, or collaboratively) to chart and alter the course of the nation for good, and in equal or greater measure, for bad.

Malaria was an insurmountable defense against a direct and lengthy occupation of West Africa beyond the coast by a large European Army, so a different approach was needed. The rank and file of an invading English colonial force had to be African. The thousands of native Hausa men streaming out of the Fuduyan Fulbe rule of their native country proved to be a readily available source.

The roots of the Nigerian Military lie in the Lagos Constabulary, also known informally as 'Glover's Hausas' which was formed in 1864. This unit was morphed and repackaged as related or successor units were set up over the next decades, to meet specific needs of the English Colonials (Government and Royal Niger Company), so names like the 'Royal Niger Company's Constabulary and the West African Frontier Force which emerged, can be put in this context.

What was clear about these forces was that while they were mostly made up of indigenes of the local colonies and protectorates (especially ethnic Hausas), these constabularies and frontier forces were set up for the interests of foreigners and non-indigenes, and were fully under their control. Some would justifiably regard today's Nigerian Army, still bearing the insignia of the invading Jihadist Foreign Fulbe Fuduyan militia, as essentially the same in spirit and purpose.

Lugard and the West African Frontier Force

The events and factors that lead to the creation of what eventually became Nigeria's military were rooted in the interests and actions of non-indigenous parties. Firstly, the Fuduyan takeover of Gobir, in Hausa Country, led to a swift herdsmen-aided takeover of the rulership of the Hausa country (city states split across the current borders of Nigeria and Niger Republic) by some Fulbe clans within a few years.

This led to a significant internal (Maguzawa) and external displacement of Hausas, especially men, all over modern-day Nigeria and other parts of West Africa.

The takeover of the political, traditional and religious leadership of Hausaland also caused a fundamental shift in the socio-economic structure of Hausaland, which led to the constant outpouring of young men from their country, and this has largely continued unabated for 220 plus years. In the decades before the formation of the Lagos Constabulary, the Alaafin of Oyo's Calvary had become almost entirely made up of Hausa men due to these phenomena, and the colonials must have picked up on this and gone for the 'lowest hanging fruit' in the composition of their forces. It also helped because due to the long history of commerce of the pre-Fulbe Hausa states, Hausa had become a second language for many non-Hausas including many parts of the area referred to as the 'Middle Belt' or 'North-Central' in post-colonial Nigeria.

A subtle, but fundamental impact of all this, was that you did not necessarily need to go to Hausa country to recruit young Hausa and Hausa speaking men.

Some of the displaced Hausas formed the bulk of the Lagos constabulary when they were formed in 1864. *Glover's Hausas* and saw action in Lagos and in the current western Nigeria and in Ghana and were a significant part of what later became the West African Frontier Force, despite the usual politics and territory-claiming that existed between the various colonial governments who were afraid of the dominance of the 'Nigerian' contingent and section of the force.

The second major factor in which Nigeria's military history is rooted is the commercial interest of England's United Kingdom (endonymically referred to as Great Britain). No man represented this more than Frederick Lugard, an officer whose promising army career had been truncated for having an affair with a married woman. Seeking redemption, and a fresh start after this shameful event, he went to East Africa (Bugandaland) and took a very different approach (semi-sanctioned armed muscle promoting English interests) to "continuing the work of David Livingstone" in East Africa.

Lugard had a get-famous-or-die-trying mentality, and the interest in the works of David Livingstone in British and Western society (or in the English-speaking world) from a few decades earlier proved to be a path of least resistance for Lugard to reverse his fall from grace and achieve the place in British high society he so desperately desired. Unlike Livingstone, Lugard had no missionary or medical interests in the service of the locals and his military background made him the ideal kind of armed muscle to force things through in the pursuit of English commercial and colonial interests.

Lugard's rumored membership of the freemason (the occult in Nigerian parlance), has also quite naturally brought spiritual and logical deductions about the role he was eventually to play in Nigeria's history.

His success and reputation as an enforcer in East Africa, led to his employment by the Royal Niger Company, which was pursuing British commercial interests in what is now Nigeria, to reprise his role in Bugandaland. Specifically, he was invited to force the French to beat a retreat from Borgu.

Lugard saw the West African Frontier Force as an army over which he would have the ultimate control and which he had been quoted as saying that it would "be employed to serve beyond Her Majesty's dominion," which was taken to mean as a mercenary force subject to his own personal desire and control. He obviously had his own agenda, which obviously had large areas of intersection with English interests, but was often aside and beyond, and did not accommodate any interference even from the colonial office.

Lugard's Borgu expedition had mixed results, with a significant part of the Borgu kingdom 'lost' to France (in the current Republic of Benin)[19]. He however veered off-course and went on a personal mission to dislodge the Fulbe Clan leaders and rulers of Hausaland, interestingly, mostly with ethnic Hausa soldiers, who had been displaced from their home country by the rule of the Fuduyan Fulbes.

Quite remarkably, some cases of direct confrontation between Lugard's WAFF and the Fulbe rulers of Hausaland and Ilorin (with Sokoto and Ilorin as notable examples) led to the flight of the rulers from these domains, which was in sharp contrast from the responses of the indigenous rulers like the Awujale in Ijebu, Jaja in Opobo and the Oba of Benin who stayed put in their kingdoms, come what may, when in direct confrontation with the English forces.

Despite the claim of wanting to remove the slave raiding Fulbe 'Emirs' (as the clan leaders refer to themselves to put a religious or Arabic hook on things) of Hausaland, Lugard restored virtually all them back to the rulership of Hausaland, with the final act being the restoration of the leadership of the Fulbe Clans to Attahiru in Sokoto, after the pursuit of the similarly named Attahiru, the incumbent leader and brother of the new leader, who had been killed in Burmi, Gombe by Lugard's pursuing forces.

For believers in matters beyond the temporal, there have been some questions about the spiritual connotations, if any, of Lugard's actions in Hausa Country as Uthman Fuduye, the leader of the Fulbe takeover of Hausaland had predicted the rulership of his clans would be displaced after a hundred years by another group of foreigners, and his Fulbe clans were to go and set up a puritan religious state by the Nile, in the Sudan, when this happened.

The Fulbe leader Attahiru must have been conflicted by Lugard's curious decision to abandon his mission in Borgu and face the Fulbe Clan leaders of Hausa land. On one hand, he knew the time was up, based on his progenitor's prediction; on the other hand though, it appears the benefits of his sovereign rule were too good to give up (even as the subjugated country got progressively poorer and desolate) and he tried to have it both ways.

He eventually sent his son Mai (W)'Urno to fulfill the ancestral directive to migrate to the banks of the Nile in Sudan, as Lugard's forces closed in on the fleeing party in current day Gombe.

COMMENTARY - APES OBEY

L et's take a brief interlude from the impactful, and nation-forging history of Nigeria's military and project about 83 years into the future from the sacking of Attahiru in Burni in 1903 to a Military School in Nigeria where two boys (IK & BJ) seemed to argue all the time over all manner of things ranging from grammar and pronunciation (how is the McVities 'TUC' biscuit pronounced anyway?) to life and living. Unlike many of their other classmates though, they didn't really discuss and argue about the nation, the military and coups. The 'barrack boys' (sons of Officers and Men of the Armed Forces) tended to do that more, given their background. It was nonetheless a life of complete immersion into the military training and mindset with endless drills, parades, weapons training, field training, route and compass marches, obstacle crossings and map reading (thankfully made obsolete by GPS) and endless runs and PT; and this was only the official part of it. We'll skip the unofficial, more-intense bits.

Quite naturally, a lot of the activity was encouraged by songs and chants, many of which most of the boys just memorized without knowing the meaning, especially since the songs were mostly in Hausa, although there were a few chants from other parts of the Nigerian State ('Enyimba Enyi' and 'Kerenke Obi' are non-Hausa staples in any Nigerian Military Cadence collection).

There was a particular chant though, that made IK & BJ get into another verbal confrontation, but which had a deeper and fundamental meaning on the history of the Nigerian Military. To BJ's ears, it sounded like 'Ehtsobey,' even though that meant nothing, but so did several other chants and songs in the military. So, when IK huddled the group of 5 one day and asked that all 5 stop responding to that particular chant (at the risk of getting into trouble, depending on the 'type of parade'), everyone waived him off as an 'ITK', even though no one from the group of 10 and 11 year olds could give an alternative meaning to counter his claim that it was a condescending colonial chant mocking the illiterate (in English) soldiers of the WAFF, by their English NCOs and Officers.

BJ thought IK might have a point, but could not get himself to accept that one group of people would mock, insult, or take advantage of another group of people, just for kicks, and right in their faces. There had to be an alternative explanation, there just had to be. Maybe it was a chant that had its origins in a minor Nigerian language, or even a foreign language (it had a South African liberation chant and vibe to it). So he asked all his 'non-WAZOBIA' classmates if 'Ehtsobey' meant anything in their language.

It didn't and it doesn't. Oftentimes (and some will argue, most of the time), the truth is the simplest and most obvious explanation, and it is staring at you, right in the face.

The fact that the indigenously peopled Frontier Force had brutally, ruthlessly and efficiently subjugated the country did not earn it respect or even basic dignity from its foreign assemblers. Quite curiously, it is suggested that Lugard, by reinstalling the Fulbe clan leaders of Hausaland, handed the country right back to another group of foreigners. It was however not Lugard's country to give in the first place; However, Fuduye's insignia still adorned the logo of the post-colonial Nigerian Army in 2024.

That is the tragedy of colonialism and allowing foreigners for whatever reason to rule over you. There will always be a reason or hook (religious, political, economic, civilization, development etc.) used to justify the takeover or occupation, but at its core is a deliberate attempt to strip a people of their independence, dignity, history, culture, freedom, way of life and to some extent part of their humanity.

Post-Amalgamation

By 1914, the West African Frontier Force, now free to operate without the constrain of Malaria, had grown to include 244 English officers, 115 English NCOs and 7,201 native officers. England's United Kingdom was now fully in control of 'Nigeria' and, the WAFF had to adjust from being an army of violent subjugation to pursuing and protecting English interests, somewhat following the path of the Fulbes clans who transitioned from violent propagations to industrial scale slave raiding and trading.

Even though the composition of the West African Frontier Force was indisputably mostly Hausa, there were some non-Hausa NCOs who had taken up leadership positions in this Force by the 1920s, perhaps due to the ability to speak the English language or their exposure to formal education. Amongst these were the highly decorated RSM Belo Akure, Belo Ojo and Inspector Ajayi, who were part of the exhibition of the British Empire in Wembley. Some have alternatively suggested that RSM Akure & Ojo may have been ethnic Hausas resident in 'Western' Nigeria from the continuous displacement from the Fulbe takeover of Hausaland. This is plausible given the Belo first names, and the tendency of Hausa to be surnamed after cities in which they reside.

RSM Belo Akure, Sgt Belo Ojo & Insp. Ajayi at the British Empire Exhibition at Wembley in 1924.

Over 45,000 Nigerian soldiers served in the Second World War, and the bravery of the Nigerian soldiers was renowned. English recruitment for the war effort was easy, at least at the beginning, with the full support of colonial mechanisms and nationalist and independence leaders like Herbert Macaulay and Nnamdi Azikiwe. A significant number of these soldiers were involved in bloody battles against the Japanese in Burma and Sri Lanka, but also played significant roles on the African continent, especially in the capture of Mogadishu (the current capital of Somalia). Nigerians also literally chased the Italians out of Ethiopia. These roles are hardly spoken of by the colonials or the countries that were liberated by the Nigerian Soldiers.

Nigerian soldiers were not even acknowledged or mentioned in the victory speech by the commanding officer, William Slim at the end of the War. Their experience was however better than that of the Senegalese soldiers who, likewise, fought on behalf of the French, and upon return to Senegal, were held in prison and gunned down in Thiaroye over protests about pay and pensions.

It is noteworthy that some of the battalions of the Nigerian Defense Academy including Abyssinia, Burma, and Mogadishu are named in commemoration of some of the exploits of Nigerian soldiers during the Second World War. It is also noteworthy that while some of the previously single campus institutions like the Nigerian Law School now have campuses spread all over the country, the Nigerian Defense Academy remains a single campus institution in Kaduna.

The use of mostly Hausa rank and file soldiers to depose and later reinstate the Fulbe rulers of Hausa Country was not lost on the ruling clans, and most especially on Ahmadu Rabbah (Bello), leader of the Northern People's Congress and defacto ruler of post-independence Nigeria, and would largely frame their opinions, thoughts, actions and approach to Nigeria's independence and the period immediately afterwards.

Rabah Bello enjoyed a rapid rise in politics, leveraging on the Fulbe control of the traditional and religious institutions in Hausaland (Nigeria's largest indigenous country), and his background as a leading member of the ruling clans. He had lost out in the effort to become the head of the clans to his relative Siddiq Abubakar, but soon found that the political process in the emerging Nigerian state was a much more effective means to exert power and control.

After their service with distinction during the 2nd World war, Nigerian soldiers started to demand for recognition and inclusion in the Officer Corps of the military, especially after further distinguished service as part of the United Nations Peacekeeping Force in Congo. Many of these soldiers, especially the southern ones, feeling a little maltreated by the British, supported the independence efforts.

Queen Elizabeth of England reviewing a Guard of Honor during a visit to Nigeria.

However, the Other Ranks (NCOs) of the military was still mostly dominated by Hausas, both from the north and those resident in the south, but with a growing role for the middle belt, especially with Tivs, Idomas, Birom and Tarok NCOs. The Officer Corps, due to the education and qualification standards required, was however dominated by Southerners, and this proved to be a huge problem for Ahmadu Bello.

First Generation of Army Officers as at June 1959

Left to right sitting: Captain Robert Adeyinka Adebayo, Captain Philip Effiong, Captain Umeh Ogere Imo, Major Samuel Adesoji Ademulegun, Major Wellington Bassey, Major General Norman Forster (GOC, Nigerian Army), Major Aguiyi Ironsi, Major Ralph Adetunji Shodeinde, Captain Zakaria Maimalari, Captain Conrad Nwawo, Captain David Akpode Ejoor. 2nd Row Standing: Lt Igboba, Lt George Remunoiyowun Kurubo, (non-Nigerian standing next to Kurubo), Lt J Akahan Akaga, Lt Patrick Awunah, Lt Louis Ogbonnia, Lt Chukwuemeka Odumegwu Ojukwu, Lt Eyo Ekpo, Lt Author Unegbe, Lt Abogo Largema. 3rd Row Standing: Lt Hillary Mbilitem Njoku, 2nd Lt Macauley Nzefili, 2nd Lt David Ogunewe, 2nd Lt Shadrack, Lt Alexander Madiebo, 2nd Lt Anthony Eze, Lt Yakubu Gowon, 2nd Lt Sylvanus Nwanjei, Lt Yakubu Pam, 2nd Lt Hassan Katsina.

Post-Independence: Quotas Over Merit

Nigeria's post-Independence Prime Minister, Abubakar Tafawa Balewa insisted that the country would stick to the principle of merit in choosing the men for the officer corps of its military. This was at complete odds with his party leader, Sir. Ahmadu Bello, who had declined to become Prime Minister, partly due to his disdain for Lagos, having failed to convince the British to move the capital to Kaduna (the feeling was mutual as Lagosians had insulted Bello as the man who kept them under British rule, when the rest of the country was ready to become independent). He promised to return to Lagos, "with a sword in his hand" when next he came in response to those insults, and Bello, and Defense Minister Muhammadu Ribadu (both of these gentlemen had an interesting past with claims of cattle rustling from their own clan members) severally pressured the Prime Minister to abandon the principle of merit in the acceptance of men to the Officer Corps of the Military, but the Prime Minister, perhaps due to his sensitivities as an indigenous Nigerian, as opposed to those putting him under pressure, stood firm and stuck to his position.

Balewa's Defense Minister, Ribadu, helped manage the sometimes-complex relationship between the Prime Minister and Ahmadu Bello. Some believe he would have found a way to avert the crisis of 1966, if he was alive. His Granddaughter, Aisha later married Muhammadu Buhari one of the boys he helped get into the military on the principle of 'stability'.

Upon the completion of the Nigerian Military (now Defense) Academy, Kaduna, Nigeria could now locally train its military officers instead of sending them to military colleges abroad. However, Ahmadu Bello was livid that many young men that he and the 'Northern' ruling class encouraged to seek admission into the academy were refused on the basis of lack of proper academic or medical fitness. Bello was very concerned that only six of Nigeria's 44 Military officers at the time were Northerners, with some of these Northerners being Christian Benue-Plateau officers.

At this point, the Prime Minister gave in to pressure, despite his previous stance about such a policy being unfair and leading to an erosion of standards. Defense Minister Ribadu's statement that "stability was at least as important as fairness" could not have been comforting to the Prime Minister.

As can be expected from actions based on such flawed thought process and logic, neither Nigeria nor its Military has had much stability, equity (fairness) or standards since then. The Army thus saw an influx of Northern officers, based on quotas meant to help the region 'catch up,' and not the regular qualification criteria for the officer corps. Several of these 'Bello-Ribadu' officers were to play leading roles in the coups, counter coups, and Military Governments (including as Heads of State) that plagued the country over the next five decades.

Ben Gbulie, Nigerian Army, and later Biafran Army Officer, gave specific examples of this impunity:

In an attempt to catch up militarily with the South, the Northern politicians had thrown out all discretion. They had lowered standards of admission drastically, settling for the minimum. For as I recalled, all the Northerners in my intake had been trained at the Mons Officer Cadet School in Aldershot. And they had become officers after barely six months of military training, whereas those of us who had been sent to Sandhurst had had to do two long years to earn the Queen's

Commission. The implications were quite clear and most disturbing. Not only had these Northerners become commissioned officers before we were half-way through our first year at Sandhurst, they had all risen to the enviable rank of Captain before we could even appear at the sovereign's parade which served essentially as a prerequisite for our passing out as Second Lieutenants.

By 1964 a group of young Nigerian officer-cadets, mostly Northerners, had been declared academically unfit and hence repatriated by the Canadian military authorities. These cadets were however pronounced commissioned by the Nigerian Federal Government no sooner than they had arrived at the Ikeja Airport. Consequently, they had had to be absorbed into the Nigerian Army as commissioned officers, even though they had received no requisite military training.

A funny side note to the Ribadu/Bello policy was that a tiny proportion of those who made it into the Army through this policy were not from the intended ethnic groups, but were able to mask their identities with assumed names, and the ability to speak Hausa, usually by virtue of being born or raised in Hausa Country.

Ribadu was extremely useful in managing the now complicated relationship between Prime Minister Balewa and his party leader and Northern Premier, Ahmadu Bello, who increasingly seemed to discount and disregard 'National' affairs and the office of the Prime Minister. He'd severally publicly state that he'd rather be Sultan of Sokoto (the lead office of the ruling Fulbe clans of Hausaland) than Prime Minister. Bello was also known to react angrily in being mistaken for being Hausa (especially in the South), and was known to angrily interrupt conversations that innocuously identified him as Hausa[20] with responses like "I am not Hausa. I'd rather be dead than be Hausa."[21]

Ribadu, as Defense Minister, oversaw the start of the Air Force and Navy, mostly through the transfer of service of regular Army Officers. A close camaraderie remains between the Officers, of all three Armed Forces as almost all the 'regular' officers are admitted and trained together for at least four years at the Nigerian Defense Academy (before the Naval Cadets head out for a final year of Sea training as Midshipmen). Ribadu also helped ensure that Kaduna (and nearby Zaria) was the focus for Nigeria's military infrastructure and institutions, except for the Navy, for obvious reasons.

Ribadu's prior experience as Minister of Land, and of Lagos affairs, meant that he was a little bit more appreciative of the needs and sensitivities of the Federal cabinet, even if his primary consideration was to his party and the Fulbe Feudalist hegemony. He, however, had a strong influence on the NPC leader, and was able to get him to change his mind when necessary and make life easier for Balewa. Ribadu's death in 1965, complicated things for Balewa especially, as his replacement as the private go between both leaders, Inua Wada, did not seem to have the same influence and persuasive qualities over Bello, who seemed increasingly more focused on his interesting religious preoccupations, many in collaboration with Abubakar Gumi, religious scholar and critic of Siddiq Abubakar. Bello performed a very public (re) conversion of Dentist and Gambian Prime Minister, David (Dauda) Jawara, a significant show of influence over the post-colonial leadership of native region and homelands of the Fuduyan Fulbes.

The normally calm and conciliatory Prime Minister was publicly quoted as saying, "I'm tired, go and tell them to do whatever they want," in frustration to another Bello move that had put him in a tight spot.

Beyond the Military History

It will probably help to broaden our perspective of the emergence of the Nigerian State from the focus on the history of its Military, and look at other critical factors, players, events, motives, decisions and institutions that helped chart the course of a Nation cobbled together for reasons that have nothing to do with the benefit of its indigenous peoples and constituent countries.

The world was a very different place at the end of the 2nd World War, and for an England that was liked saved from German occupation by a combination of American involvement and the soldiers from its colonies (almost 1.5 million from India alone), the Indian Independence Act of 1947 was a huge problem.

The fear and possibility of a 3rd World War was very real at this time, and the lack of access to 1.5 million troops that could be called from newly independent India meant the English Colonials needed an 'insurance policy' from where a million or two million troops could be quickly assembled and trained for its service if needed. The place that best fit this profile in the British Empire was Hausa Country under the Fuduyan Fulbe rule.

Most of the men in the Lagos Constabulary that transformed to 'Glover's Hausas' and the West African Frontier Force, were ethnic Hausas, as were a significant number of the

45,000 'Nigerians' that served in World War 2 (WW2). If the English Colonials could get this number of Hausas without a direct and aggressive recruitment in Hausaland, then they could definitely get a million or two if directly collaborating with the Fuduyan Fulbe rulers of Hausaland.

It was unlikely that any other part of Nigeria would offer her sons as cannon fodder for the English cause, and Hausaland under the rule of indigenous Hausas would have been a big gamble. It was thus important that Hausaland remained under the rule of the foreign Fulbe clans. In this regard, Lugard's decision to re-install the Fulbe Clan leaders in Hausaland 40 plus years earlier proved fortuitous, and possibly strategic, though it is unlikely that it was planned for this purpose, but it can't be ruled out as the war mongering European powers were on the verge of WW1 at this time.

Taking aggressive self-preservatory decisions was not uncommon for the English, during and in the period after the 2nd World War. For instance, Churchill (through his Secretary of State for Colonial Office, one of the sources quoted in the 'From the Horse's Mouth' section of this book) offered to cede Northern Ireland to Ireland, if Ireland abandoned its stance of neutrality and joined WW2 on the English side. Ireland however declined thinking that keeping most of Ireland Irish, was better than losing all of Ireland (and the United Kingdom) to Germany, which was common thought at the time, before the entrance of the United States into WW2 in December 1941.

This mindset of the English towards Nigeria, also led to the concentration of military training and the bulk of military activity to Kano and Zaria in the heart of Hausa Country and

Kaduna, on the fringe of Hausa Country, which became the capital of Nigeria's northern protectorate and region.

From the Horse's Mouth

This section looks at official transcripts and records of the conversations, opinions, thoughts and motives of High-level Colonial and English officials on the events and personalities of 'Pre-Independence' Nigeria.

They are sourced from the 'British End of the Empire Project,' edited by Martin Lynn.

While the English agenda evolved as decades passed, it was still for the benefit of England at each point in time, and not in the interest of the countries constituted as Nigeria, or their indigenes.

Studying and knowing the intent and design of the creator, is essential in understanding the performance, function or malfunction of the product or creation.

Official English Colonial records in Italics, BN comments highlighted.

Evidence that the English Colonials set up Bello's invitation to the Action Group in 1952.

July 1958

[Political situation]: minutes by M G Smith, A Emanuel, Sir J. Macpherson, and Lord Perth on the implications of the NPC-NCNC alliance.

According to the Secretary of State.

I am usually optimistic about Nigeria but I confess that these and other recent developments have caused me to share to some extent Mr. Maurice Smith's gloom. It would have been very easy for the Action Group to make friends with the N.P.C. at any time in the past six or seven years. I tried very hard to try to persuade them to do so, and also to back the 'good' Easterners who were then on the Council of Ministers and who broke with Zik (Nwapa Arikpo and Eni Njoku). The Action Group utterly refused, and played straight into Ziks hands when they caused the crisis in 1953—at a time when the North, the West and the good 'East' were all opposed to Zik and his disreputable crowd. The N.P.C. were not blameless in failing to play with the Action Group but they had ample proof of the latter's faithlessness. At that time, the Action Group was chauvinistically Yoruba. I do not know whether Awolowo was ever then planning for power in the ghout Nigeria. He is now becoming statesmanlike but he is now definitely planning for such power, and will invade Action Group through the East and the North in the Federal elections. I ruefully agree with the last sentence of Mr. Emanuel's minute. J.S.M. 30.7.58 Gloomy—but is there nothing we can do? The Constitutional Conference will be interesting

With the inevitability of Independence apparent, Zik agreed to go to Centre as the Governor-General, believing that he would wield the same control over the Armed Forces that the last (colonial) Governor-General did. That turned out to be a miscalculation, although the requirement that the Governor-General had to invite the Prime Minister to form a government proved to be an asset for him after the messy 1964 elections.

Prime Minister Tafawa Balewa was universally respected, even though he seemed to set a pattern of Nigerian leaders who are 'good people' but are, unfortunately, too weak or lack the vision to change the bad system in which they find themselves. Hence, they can't do much to alter the faulty platforms that propped them into the office. These 'good guys' lack the ability, drive or will power to push needed change. Tafawa Balewa, for instance, seemed convinced by the long-standing colonial belief that Nigeria's best chance probably laid with the Action Group running the country but without the Political Power, as the junior member in a coalition. Also, he apparently desired to have Awolowo as Deputy Prime Minister, although there is little evidence that this would have improved the fundamentally flawed Nigerian state significantly.

Observing Ahmadu Bello outside the perspective of Hausaland's foreign Fulbe Hegemony (that also believes it has the guardianship of the Nigerian State) will only fuel images of a disturbing influence and factor on the already faulty and fractured Nigerian Nation.

Nobody, however, deserves to be murdered in cold blood, regardless of your thoughts and perspectives on their person or role.

Bello, and the members of his Fulbe ruling clans were extremely crucial to fulfilling England's refined colonial objective for Nigeria at the end of the WW2. India's Independence meant the Fulbe control of Hausaland was England's assurance for ground troops in the case a third world war broke out. Indeed, they needed the rest of Nigeria to make the arrangement sustainable, since the ruling clans had 'progressively' destroyed the Hausa economy over their century-long rule.

The English Colonials were, however, very happy to work with Ahmadu Bello in what was effectively a mutually beneficial coalition of foreigners to the detriment of the indigenous countries and peoples of Nigeria.

The mutual need or benefit did not translate to respect however, as official and unofficial communications on Bello show.

'Nigeria': Cabinet memorandum by Mr. Lennox-Boyd on the current situation

At the 1957 Conference I agreed to the creation of an office of Federal Prime Minister and to an all-Nigerian Federal Council of Ministers presided over by the Governor-General, whose members would be appointed by the Governor-General on the Prime Minister's recommendation. The United Kingdom interest was secured by the agreement of the Conference that the Governor-General should retain until independence his general reserved powers to act without consulting his Ministers or against their advice, and his responsibility, in his discretion, for external affairs and defense, for the use of and operational control of the Police and for the Federal Public Service.

The leader in the Federal Legislature of the Northern People's Congress, Alhaji Abubakar Tafawa Balewa, became the first Federal Prime Minister and sought to create a 'national' government to work for early independence by including in his team Ministers from the Action Group, who are the dominant party in the West but weak in the Federal Legislature, in addition to members of the National Council of Nigeria and the Cameroons (N.C.N.C.), the major party in the East, and of his own party, the Northern People's Congress (N.P.C.). The Prime Minister is sagacious and able and relations between him and the Governor-General are frank and cordial. He is openly anti-Communist, he is under no illusions about the difficulties of the task facing both himself and the country, and his policy is likely to be as pro-Western as the narrow Muslim outlook of his principal Northern supporters will allow. (In his party hierarchy he is only deputy to the leader, the vain and pompous Sardauna of Sokoto, Premier of the Northern Region).

Perceptions of Bello by the English outside of their official colonial circles were probably poorer, as English historian John Iliffe describes.

Accepting with regret the need to participate in party politics, he nevertheless considered democratic competition beneath his dignity, outlawing it in his constituency and leaving interparty bargaining to 'young kids'. He saw politics rather as patronage, appointing ministers without consulting them and treating close civil servants as junior members of his family. Yet qualities deemed 'vain and pompous' by the British won admiration in the north. 'He was always superbly dressed,' it was recalled, 'and the sight of him, and the glittering cortege of large American cars that accompanied him, never failed to please a people that loved display for its own sake.' The crowds delighted in his ostentatious and reckless munificence, which thronged his house with supplicants and threw him into debt, which his bank discreetly cancelled.

There was unfavorable correspondence on Zik. The colonials were apparently willing to take drastic action, including banning and jailing him, but they were worried about the reaction of America and India, as well as the possibility of boosting Zik's image.

The English Colonials deeply despised Zik. The reasons include the American factor and the Ghana sedition case. More so, Zik did not fit into their plans for Fuduyan-Fulbe control of Nigeria. He believed NCNC could win in the West & East, so he was not keen to work with Awolowo, or have Adelabu run as NCNC leader in West, which was a strategy that might have pushed the party over the hump. There was, however, some credibility to the suggestion that he had an excellent talk but did not have the interest to walk the walk of governance.

'Nigeria': Cabinet memorandum by Mr. Lennox-Boyd on the current situation

In the East, government has seriously run down. Dr. Azikiwe ('Zik'), leader of the N.C.N.C. remains in power as the personification of Ibo tribalism, but his chronic unwillingness to tolerate around him men of independence of mind has brought into being a Regional Executive Council, almost all of whom are nonentities. Some of the Federal Ministers drawn from his party, notably Dr. Mbadiwe, have recently lost their posts through constant but so far ineffective warfare against his personal dictatorship of party affairs. His star may be on the wane. At present he has no serious rival as leader of the Ibos, who are much the largest race in the Region, and although it would be much healthier for Nigeria if his hand were removed from the helm, the time has passed when H.M. Government could take any effective action to hasten this process. He must be left to the disillusionment of his own people.

The Action Group expected to win in the West, and it did without the falsely assumed cross-carpeting, but English Colonials were terrified about the possibility of Zik taking control of both Southern regions. They considered taking drastic measures to prevent or delay self-government including banning the NCNC.

We also have anecdotal evidence that Hausaland was meant to be a major source of troops to fight the English course, in case there was a WW3.

Sir J. Rankine's present view is that the Action Group will win this, but it is always possible that this may be wrong and the N.C.N.C. will emerge in control of both Regions.

The Governor says that if British officers go on self-government, chaos will occur within two years. Many of us are of the opinion that the only feasible way now to stop British officers going on self-government is by political action. I agree that on present form and advice suspension of the constitution is impracticable; but the minimum political action which I believe we can take to prevent chaos is suspension of the promise of regional self-government in 1956. We now have much less time in which to maneuver. The sands are nearly run out.

June 1955

[Eastern Region crisis]: letter (reply) from Sir C Pleass to T B Williamson on the possibility of an administrative breakdown in the Eastern Region. Minutes by M G Smith, T B Williamson, C G Eastwood, Sir T Lloyd and Mr. Hopkinson

We should hold back self-government from the East for a minimum of three years from 1956 (though I doubt whether any period should be mentioned even as a minimum). The North would be relieved; and the lesson would not be lost on the West who would be on their best behavior lest it should 'happen here.' Not everything is against us. The African respects strength. Hence Zik's great respect for Lord Chandos, and his publicly expressed preference for him over Mr. Creech-Jones at a meeting in London after the 1953 conference (with Mr. Fen-

ner Brockway in the chair). Hence too Mr. Awolowo's quiet (if temporary) acceptance of H.M.G.'s decision on Lagos after Lord Chandos had informed him, in reply to his threats of violence, that any attempt to alter H.M.G.'s decision on Lagos by force would be resisted. 'Black man like strong word.' Zik is a coward. He will be brave to rouse the rabble, but will leave others to deal with the police. He is also a twister. Despite his fair words and perfect manners, he should never be trusted. **The military and strategic position has changed. Most of the advice given from this Department in the last few years has been based on the assumption that we must at almost all costs have West Africa on our side in the event of a third world war.** The latest expert military appreciations show that this thinking is now out of date. **Moreover, world prices for many of Nigeria's important exports are falling.**

As the Governor again says Zik must never be made a martyr and unless we could be fairly sure of this the card would probably not be worth playing.

June 1955

[Eastern Region crisis]: letter (reply) from Sir C Pleass to T B Williamson on the possibility of an administrative breakdown in the Eastern Region. Minutes by M G Smith, T B Williamson, C G Eastwood, Sir T Lloyd and Mr. Hopkinson

Zik is much too astute a politician to give us good grounds for suspending the Constitution, unless he himself wished us to suspend it, in which case it would clearly not be to our advantage to fall in with his wish. If it were his wish that the Constitution should be suspended, he would of course be delighted if we did that without adequate grounds for our action, since this would *give him an opportunity to pose as a martyr not only before his own people but also before America and India.*

There is no basis for the Nigerian State outside of English Colonial and Foreign Fulbe interests. Note that the dislike by 'the North' here means the foreign Fulbe rulers of Hausaland. Their word is law in Hausa country, due to the firm control of all the institutions of authority. Indigenous Nigerian communities have had dealings with each other for centuries without the structure of the Nigerian State. Borgu, Nupe and Oyo were probably more connected regions than Oyo and Ijebu, for instance.

Also, neither the Igalas, the Idomas, Tivs nor any of the so-called northern minorities had any fear of Southern domination, and it is ridiculous to even suggest that ethnic groups gerrymandered into 'the North' by Lugard would have some phantom fear of domination by the South.

The English also have an overrated view of their performance. Firstly, the colonial adventure in Nigeria, which started out as shameless European plundering, was fully transactional, even at its best, as the goals and objectives changed over time. The regions had to be profitable, even after accounting for the cost of the military, and the wages of the colonial officers, and the cost of any infrastructure and projects.

Naturally, not much was achieved. There were very few schools and Hospitals, and there was no mass literacy or development programs outside what was needed to entrench and sustain colonial interests. Hence, the rail lines ran North to South (towards the Coasts) to facilitate the extraction of resources from the country. The focus was on getting resources out of the country, and later for 'Military Insurance' for England.

So much more was achieved in less than a decade, when there was some sort of competence in Governance in the Western region of Nigeria, for example, before that Government was aggressively taken down.

July 1958

'Nigeria': Cabinet memorandum by Mr. Lennox-Boyd on the current situation

Educational progress is still slow and there is no prospect for a generation of the Region being able to replace from its own resources the overseas officers who have served them so well. The North fears and dislikes the more educated Southerners and if they were not economically bound to the Federation would be glad to be quit of it.

Reports by M G Smith, A Emanuel, Sir J Macpherson, and Lord Perth, Reporting on the implications of the NPC-NCNC alliance for the elections leading up to Independence.

Dr. Azikiwe chose to go to the Centre as Governor-General (later President), perhaps reluctant to be in an alliance of equals with the Action Group and believing (or hoping) the role would have command of the Military as it did under the English Governor-General. He was wrong!

July 1958

[Political situation]: minutes by M G Smith, A Emanuel, Sir J Macpherson, and Lord Perth on the implications of the NPC-NCNC alliance

Last month at the Sardauna's invitation Dr. Azikiwe visited him in Kaduna and it appeared at least likely that the visit had led to an alliance between the parties concerned to fight next year's Federal elections not openly as allies but with the minimum of inconvenience to each other and with the object of creating a coalition to exclude the Action Group from power. This alliance was specifically confirmed by Sir Ralph Grey's record below (117) of a talk he had with the Prime Minister. It would seem that the N.P.C. are not confident of their ability to win an outright majority at next year's election and have decided that they must choose one of the other major parties as allies.

They have chosen the N.C.N.C., not because they have lost their dislike for it but because internal weakness and division makes it an easier ally than the Action Group. The N.P.C. will at least hope to manage the N.C.N.C. while they might find themselves managed by the big guns of the Action Group.

Furthermore, while in the past the N.C.N.C. and the Ibos who support them have been a threat in the North, over the past 12 months the major threat has come from the considerable organizing ability and financial resources of the Action Group. This has led to the troubles in Ilorin and to the general Action Group campaign in alliance with the United Middle Belt Congress to win seats throughout the Middle Belt areas.

What we have not had confirmed is the statement in the last paragraph of the Manchester Guardian article that Dr. Azikiwe proposed at next year's elections to go to the center. The inertia he has displayed these last two years would suggest that this is unlikely. But he still might be tempted there by the prospect of the power at the center that independence will bring. No doubt the N.P.C. will continue to provide the Prime Minister in the person of Abubakar, but the latter's popularity and position in his party is by no means secure (see the Deputy Governor North's letter at (41) on WAF/103/3/01 below).

Dr. Azikiwe's crumbling fortunes may well have been re-stored by this assurance of power following next year's elections and he may be looking forward to taking his place on the African and world stage beside Dr. Nkrumah, if not as Prime Minister at least as Foreign Minister of Nigeria. This might give him just the scope for vague but popular speech-making that he most enjoys, divorced from the detail of internal administration which clearly he dislikes.

On their fears over the soon to be Independent Nigeria and the fact that the Action Group, who they hoped would run the Country, but not have the Political Power were now out in the cold.

July 1958

[Political situation]: minutes by M G Smith, A Emanuel, Sir J Macpherson, and Lord Perth on the implications of the NPC-NCNC alliance

In the Federation the Prime Minister himself has both quality and integrity. Chief Festus (with overseas officers to do the work) makes a bluff and cheerful Minister of Finance. The 2 Action Group members are competent and Dr. Mbadiwe manages to get by. Only in the West is there a team of Ministers with genuine experience and ability able to guide their civil servants and to direct the business of the Region, but these men and their colleagues now at the Centre are to be excluded from Federal office.

There are a very few senior African officers of any value in the East and the best of these, Udoji, has recently been handsomely and publicly victimized by Dr. Azikiwe & has asked to retire with compensation

However optimistic one tries to be, it is difficult, taking things at best, not to be greatly concerned at the prospect of independence in about two years' time for so large and divided and inexperienced a country as Nigeria. Now that it seems likely that the best brains and experience in Nigeria—the leaders of the Action Group—are to be excluded from power, our concern must be much greater. To apply a famous saying to Nigerian independence——I don't know whether it will frighten the Nigerians, but by Heaven it frightens me

Azikwe, the NYM and Pre-Indepedence

"Kofo goes to school and all hell breaks loose," might be an appropriate title for an article or satire about the crises that plagued the Nigerian Youth Movement (previously and more appropriately named the *Lagos Youth Movement*) in 1939.

Dr Kofo Abayomi was returning to the UK for graduate studies in Surgery and as such, his position as head of the Nigerian Youth Movement (NYM) and as a Lagos city councilman would be vacant. The movement had surprised all, including itself, earlier when it featured candidates for the Lagos City Council and got elected to three of the positions.

Ernest Ikoli, an Ijaw gentleman was elected as president of the Movement and was expected to take the seat occupied by the outgoing president of the movement, Kofo Abayomi, on the Lagos City Council, in line with its own guidelines. This was however unacceptable to Dr. Nnamdi Azikiwe, editor and publisher of the West African Pilot. Azikiwe returned to Lagos only two years earlier but had already become an influential member, even if not a ranking member of the movement, so he backed (pushed) Samuel Akinsanya instead to take up the position in the Lagos City Council.

Dr. Nnamdi Azikiwe, Oba Samuel Akinsanya

Samuel (later Oba) Akinsanya was a jolly good fellow, educated, but not to the same degree as most of the leadership of the NYM, but he had major 'street credibility.' He was leader of the transport union (think of a more polished version of MC Oluomo or any of the current Transport Union and Park Overlords). In addition to this, he was also Organizing Secretary of the Nigerian Produce Trader's Union. The impact of commodities in the Nigeria of the 30's will make this second role similar to the headship of a combined NUPENG and PENGASSAN (Petroleum Unions) or even the Labor Union.

Zik realized the significant leverage that the "street" could bring, especially combined with his growing media influence, and launched an audacious takeover attempt of the Union through Akinsanya.

Zik was a man in a hurry, and he would not allow a bunch of tea-sipping, English educated socialites stand in his way.

Dr Nnamdi Azikiwe, extremely determined to achieve his goals, strived to make the most of whatever situation he found himself. For instance, he was so determined to go to America that he reportedly stowed away on a ship before he was discovered and dropped off in Ghana. He didn't bemoan his fate but took up work in Ghana and was working his way up to save money before he was called back to Nigeria and his father eventually sent him to America.

Zik worked a number of menial jobs, and he was a very resourceful person. He attended two historically black colleges (HBCUs) and two Ivy League colleges. This got him exposed to a diverse range of experiences, enhancing his ability to be resourceful. There are not very many people who claim, even today, that they attended two Ivy League colleges and two HBCUs. Added to this fact is that he had lived in many parts of the country: he was born in Zungeru, and he studied in Onitsha, Calabar and Lagos. Indeed, Zik was a man of many parts and places.

The fact that he also schooled in America rather than the UK made him one-of-a-kind, even among the nationalists. His experience and worldview were very much different from those of not just the leaders of the Nigerian nationalist movement and professionals, but also from those of the colonial authorities and officers. Perhaps, these divergent worldviews brought a certain level of distrust that several people in the Nigerian Independence movement and the Colonials had for Azikiwe. Maybe it was just a lack of understanding, but he also had a bit of a reputation for starting trouble but not being around to deal with the consequences. Maybe it was just a case of his writing being more militant than his personality.

In addition to Zik's recognition of the streets, media and transport unions to politics, (something a certain Bola Tinubu and other politicians would wake up to several decades later), Zik also seemed determined to stop the election of Ernest Ikoli, a rival journalist, an Ijaw (Izon) gentleman, and non-Afeire[22] to the house because it might have an impact on his own prospects down the line for whatever reason.

Samuel Akinsanya, Zik's proxy, left politics all together shortly afterwards and two years later, became the Oba of his own town, Is(h)ara, reigning from 1941 to 1985. So, it seemed quite unlikely that he was even more interested in politics. Akinsanya was noted for referring to the two Action Group rebels Ladoke Akintola and Remi Fani-Kayode as "misguided small boys." They, in turn, reduced his salary to 1 penny per annum.

Zik's return to Lagos from Ghana was hastened by an overturned conviction for sedition for a controversial article published in the African Morning Post. He was the editor of the paper but not the article's author. After he absolved himself of responsibility for the article, his conviction was overturned, and he started the West African Pilot in Lagos. The Pilot soon became quite successful and Zik had a conglomerate of newspapers and businesses all over the country within a decade. This media influence made Zik a popular figure in the Nigerian Youth Movement and the ensuing crisis should be viewed in this light.

After failing to get Akinsanya to take Kofo Abayomi's vacated seat, Zik (or as reported, but unlikely, Akinsanya through Zik's newspapers) would bizarrely claim that the Movement (that had just elected an Ijaw as its President, and to the Lagos Council) was discriminating against Ijebu-Afeires, and his own ethnic Igbos. This led to a split in the movement, with Zik taking most of the Igbo members out of the movement and thus establishing a solid base with which he would form a partnership with the aging Herbert Macaulay, who had been knocked off the political scene by the NYM, a few years later.

It was not the last time that Zik would leave a trail of confusion when not able to have his way. Obafemi Awolowo, an Ijebu-Afeire himself, was clearly not impressed with Zik, or his methods.

For most of the 30s, the NYM, which was more of a league of educated African professionals and intellectuals in the city, got on very well with the English Governor-General Bourdillon, who believed that nationalism was understandable, but needed to be managed. Bourdillon was somewhat impressed by the professional cadre of the members of the movement and the surprising gains they had pulled in the Council elections. Thus, he was quite friendly with the ranking members; Azikiwe even became his tennis partner.

Perhaps due to his friendliness with Bourdillon, Azikiwe and members of the youth movement supported the English war effort in World War II, especially since there were unfounded rumors that Nigeria was to be ceded to the Nazis either if England lost, or by the British to appease Nazi Germany.

Zik and six other editors were invited to the UK in 1943 on a trip sponsored by the British council to view life in England in general and especially during the war.

The British government assigned a chaperone, a colonial information officer, to the journalists, and he documented his thoughts on Zik. He thought that Zik:

- Was sincere in his opinion but unscrupulous in his way of getting them across.
- Was a very clever man but used to skating on thin ice.
- Had excellent manners but was not trusted by the other editors.

Again, these thoughts might have been the English perception of the American background and personality in general, but these thoughts cannot be completely discounted.

Bourdillon retired from the colonial office shortly afterwards and was replaced by a man who was said to have had a mindset of subduing nationalism. But again, that was probably in line with the British policy at the time of ensuring that they had to be able to get a couple of million troops out of Hausa country if there was ever a third world war. A nationalism-subduing policy was therefore required.

This, however, got Zik a bit more frustrated and his writing became more militant, as opposed to the conciliatory and supportive nature it had towards the colonials during WWII.

It was said around this time that Zik's writing helped radicalize, at least, from the English perspective, the nationalist movement, with the Zikist movement and its revolutionary undertones, emerging, and the NCNC started pushing for constitutional reforms. Zik and the NCNC wrongly assumed that Nigeria was not a league of forced countries and opposed the rights of regions to secede.

Zik supported the general strike of 1945, while Ladoke Akintola, a journalist and former teacher at the Baptist Academy, opposed the strike. Some suggest Akintola was used by the English Colonials for their interests and agenda throughout his time on the Nigerian political scene, and this narrative gained traction and credibility as the 36-year-old Akintola, already a leading journalist, got an English scholarship to study law in 1946.

This was the basis of the rivalry and suspicion between Akintola and the young Anthony Enahoro who was editor of Nnamdi Azikiwe's paper, the Southern Nigerian Defender. The paper was established in Warri, but its office was later moved to Ibadan in 1944.

Zik and the colonials both had a trust and timing problem. Regarding the timing, the 1940s and 1950s just seemed to drag on forever for Zik who believed that he ticked all the boxes to be the post-war and post-independence leader of Nigeria. But the English definitely had issues, at least, in the 40s and early 50s with an independent Nigeria (due the 'Insurance policy that Hausa Country provided, with the reality of an Independent India). They suggested that it would take a generation to grant independence, not the maximum of 15 years after the war that Zik had suggested.

Even though the colonials did not think that Zik would resort to subversive or revolutionary activities or militancy, they were worried enough about his writing and ventures and decided that neither he, nor the NCNC would play a part in their plans and arrangements for Nigeria.

This explains the continuous pressure on Awolowo and the Action Group to go into an alliance with the NPC, a suggestion that Awolowo consistently rejected for over a decade. It seemed Akintola and Fani-Kayode were, however, a tiny but significant minority in the AG leadership in this regard.

Zik's pathway to Nigeria's leadership was straightforward and simple. He had the East on lockdown and only needed to pull an upset in the West; he did not need an alliance, and had been strategizing for this since the orchestrated NYM split of the 30's. Awolowo and the Action Group had a different approach, wanting to go into an alliance on its own strength and not as a junior partner. Hence, it needed to secure the West and form alliances with other indigenous Nigerians that it felt were under the oppression of foreign Fuduyan Fulbes, hence its push into the Middle Belt.

Whether real or imagined, the colonials also felt that Zik was dictatorial as well as poor with administration and details, which is hard to believe of a former editor. But maybe Zik had just become tired of waiting for what he thought was his, after two and half decades of activism without independence. The colonials also believed that they had enough in terms of infractions to jail him and proscribe the NCNC. However, they were afraid of international reactions, especially from the USA where Zik had a large base of friends and support as well as the newly independent India. Thus, they decided not to arrest him or proscribe the NCNC, believing that if they were able to push through the Action Group and NPC alliance, Zik would naturally fade into obscurity.

With this background in mind, it was surprising to most observers, including the English Colonials, that Zik pulled the joker and went into an alliance with the Ahmadu Bello led Northern People's Congress for the 1959 elections leading up to Nigeria's independence. It appeared that Zik assumed that his NCNC would have equal powers with the NPC under this arrangement. He also thought that, as Governor-General, he would have control of the military, just as the outgoing English Governor-General did. This, however, proved to be a gross miscalculation and despite Zik's attempt to force the position of the Governor-General and later President into that of a Commander-in Chief.

The limitations of the powers of the office proved to be a source of great frustration for Dr Nnamdi Azikiwe. This played a huge part as things blew up and eventually it degenerated into civil war.

Akintola and the Failed NPC-AG Alliance

There may have been markers from the past to suggest the controversial role that Akintola was going to play in the Action Group's (and eventually Nigeria's) crisis. However, there was no indication from Remi Fani-Kayode's background of the fact that he would be Akintola's co-traveler in that process.

Born in England in 1921, Remi Fani-Kayode had completed his law degree by his early 20s. He went on to co-found the law firm Thomas, Williams & Kayode with Bode Thomas and Rotimi Williams. Boasting a privileged background, he had no reason to be intimidated by or beholden to the English colonials. If anything at all, like Bode Thomas, Awolowo, Enahoro, Jakande, Chike Obi and the rest of Action Group stalwarts, he was expected to combine his education and cultural pride to pursue home-grown solutions and aggressive development policies.

However, like Akintola, he was also expected to know that the English colonials trying to force an alliance between the Action Group and the NPC could not have been working for the good of their people or region.

After the 1966 coups, he withdrew from Nigeria and the political scene for some time, but would reemerge late in the 1970s, serving as the vice-chairman of the Fulbe led National Party of Nigeria that produced President Shehu Shagari. He also famously formed a law firm with Sobo Sowemimo, the brother of the judge that jailed the Action Group leadership (about 27 of them) in 1963. The Judge, George Sowemimo, was appointed as the Chief Justice of Nigeria, by President Shagari in 1983.

Remi Fani-Kayode and Shehu Shagari

Fani-Kayode's motivation for his actions and decisions can hardly be explained by a quest for political ascendancy or wealth. Perhaps some undisclosed issues the now-defunct Thomas, Williams & Kayode or a hold by the English colonials that hasn't come to light may be responsible.

To be fair, in the 1960 - 1965 period, each of the major parties was deeply interested in not just consolidating its base but grabbing new frontiers. The Action Group, which had spent the previous decade refusing colonial pressure to merge or ally with the NPC, certainly felt slighted that significant parts of Afeire Country and affiliated ethnicities, including Ilorin, Kabba, Offa, and Igala Country were gerrymandered to the 'North'. Members of the party felt that with some effort, these places could be regained and reinstated (at least politically) into the Western Region. They probably also felt that there was no basis for the foreign Fulbe control of neighboring indigenous areas, which was what Ahmadu Bello's leadership of the NPC represented. This drove the partnership with Joseph Tarka and the United Middle Belt Congress.

Also, the AG leaders believed in true federalism and ideologically didn't consider a strong alliance necessarily. However, the party expressed its willingness to enter into an alliance with Nnamdi Azikiwe's NCNC if it became necessary. Thus, it seemed that the AG leaders were not entirely opposed to forging alliances with other parties; they only wanted to do so from a position of strength.

On the other hand, Dr. Azikiwe thought he and his party could go solo and gain a majority of federal seats if only they could win the Western region. Such an assumption was not as far-fetched as it seemed. Azikiwe had the power of the media, and he believed that by forming strategic partnerships with influential figures (which it didn't do, with great vigor or much success), the NCNC could defeat the Action Group in the west while retaining its Eastern region domination.

Already, the circumstances of the Action Group's emergence were already a problem for Azikiwe. The party materialized out of the socio-cultural group, Egbe Afenifere in 1951. Before then, Azikiwe was confident that the NYM palava (caused by him) was only a slight bump on his path to the leadership of a Nigerian state that would be Africa's most populous. Maybe it was even a statement of intent. This explains his irritation with the Action Group, especially since there was virtually no threat to his hold on the East; the West was the problem.

On his part, Ahmadu Bello, a Fulbe aristocrat, believed that with the English colonial support, that he would dominate the country in one way or another. As such, when the colonials proposed that the NPC allied with the Action Group, he was open to the idea, since conquest could be by Violent Propagation, Slave raids, and administrative arrangements like junior alliances in politics, or other arrangements like RUGA or farming settlements.

He never really got over losing an attempt at the leadership of the Fuduyan Fulbe Clans to his relative Siddique Abubakar, but embraced the means of the colonial Nigerian State as a means to achieve his objectives, following the colonial rescue from an attempt by clan leader and relative, Siddique, to jail him over real or imagined infractions having to do with cattle.

Bello soon assumed political leadership of Hausa country, and the gerrymandered North through the NPC, and also tried to create an alternative religious authority to clip the wings of his rival and clan leader, in partnership with Fulbe religious scholar, Abubakar Gumi.

Bello often used shocking language (and seemed determined to back it up, with the TIV situation and the Action Group crisis being examples) pertaining to slaves, swords and even conquered Hausa Country, and clearly identified his clan as foreigners, who similar to (or in partnership with) the English Colonials "owned" the emerging Nigerian State.

The world shifted a bit between 1950 and 1965. Fears of a third world war soon gave way to the Cold War. The English colonials, historically and institutionally, maintained strong support for the NPC and Ahmadu Bello, but this was based on mutual self-interest.

It was therefore not surprising to experienced observers that as the first military coup happened, the British declined to intervene militarily (or even acknowledge the request from the scrambling NPC politicians), choosing instead to sit back and watch where the pendulum of power would swing; whoever emerged winner would have English support.

After all, their policy in the earlier part of the previous 15 years had been to ensure that they could get out the troops to fight British battles for the English cause. They were definitely not prepared to have British soldiers and lives lost for the Fuduyan Fulbe cause in Nigeria. That would be the complete opposite of their objectives, plans, and strategy.

Aguiyi-Ironsi quickly schemed his way to seize control over the country amidst the confusion. A move with bad intentions, which was badly managed (even if it had a brief facade of a smooth operator), and one that had very bad consequences.

It Takes Two to Bring the House Down

Ladoke Akintola was very different from the younger partners from privileged backgrounds in the law firm Thomas, Williams & Kayode. Their parents could afford an education at the best universities in the UK and the young men returned to Nigeria in their 20s to set up a law firm. On the other hand, Akintola had to 'earn' everything the hard way. He could only attend law school after he had crossed over to journalism after a long teaching career at the Baptist Academy.

As a journalist, he opposed the Azikiwe and the NCNC strike in 1945. That also put him in direct opposition with the very young Anthony Enahoro, who was the editor of Zik's newspaper, and continued to view Akintola with suspicion and distrust, even as they were ranking members in the Action Group. Akintola and Ahmadu Bello had a particular dislike for Enahoro, and the soon to be deceased Bode Thomas, and put pressure on the English Colonials to extradite Enahoro, who had escaped the mass crackdown on the Action Group Leadership through Ghana, before eventually ending up in England.

After Akintola's English funded scholarship to study law, he returned to Nigeria and worked under the younger partners before crossing over to link up with Dr Chris Ogunbanjo in another law firm. He also dipped his feet into politics, initially as a legal adviser to the Action Group.

Perhaps all these young men would have lived much wealthier and less stressful lives if they had just remained in private law practice. Rotimi Williams became one of Nigeria's foremost lawyers, with a glorious career that spanned over 6 decades. He was to Nigerian law what his brother, Akintola Williams was to Nigerian accounting: a doyen. Chris Ogunbanjo had a similar impact in law. Rightly or wrongly, these young men were attracted by politics, perhaps motivated by a desire to help build the emerging nation, or just a self-serving desire to be the ones 'running things.'

Akintola's supporters have tried to play down his part in this crisis that soon overran the Action Group, and the rest of Nigeria, by suggesting that having grown up in Minna, on the border of Nupe and Hausa countries, his perspective was a bit different from the rest of his party stalwarts. The fact that he spoke Hausa fluently (he also spoke Nupe) meant that he could relate with Ahmadu Bello a bit more intimately (the Fulbe ruling class adopted Hausa as their secondary language in addition to their native Fulfulde). Akintola, reportedly, helped bring Ahmadu Bello and co back to the table following the continual walkouts staged every time the Action Group raised a motion for Nigeria's independence.

Maybe he deserves some credit in that regard, but it probably would have made sense if questions about Nigeria's future and the differences between the various constituent indigenous countries have been emphasized and settled at that point. Instead, bringing everyone back only meant making collective decisions that served nobody's interest at the end of the day.

Following the death of Bode Thomas at the young age of 34. Akintola and the Alaafin (Adeyemi) decided to symbolically dance on his grave with their actions afterwards. Bode Thomas, Lagos born, held the high non-royal title of *Balogun* of Oyo and shortly after his death, the Alaafin Adeyemi II appointed Akintola as the Aare Ona Kakanfo, which was not an Oyo title but one that represented the traditional field marshal of the entire Afeire Confederacy. The office had been unoccupied for about 80 years since Latoosa of Ibadan.

In addition, Akintola contested to replace the late Bode Thomas as deputy leader of the Action Group, and despite Awolowo's obvious preference for Chief Arthur Prest, Akintola had his way with the strong support of Fani-Kayode.

Akintola and Fani-Kayode may have reasoned that their actions could reverse the fortunes of the party following its loss in the federal elections of 1953, which was due to the unpopular taxes that were introduced to finance free primary Education and Healthcare. The Alaafin was particularly opposed to this tax, both because he felt it increased the burden on his people and limited the role of his Native Authority. Bode Thomas, Awolowo's Man Friday, and major proponent of the party policies, was now at odds with his Alaafin, who was openly campaigning for the opposition NCNC.

L: Fani-Kayode with Akintola R: Bode Thomas, Awolowo and Akintola

However, it soon became obvious that the taxes were being put to good use as the region had shot ahead of other parts of the country in development, education, and free healthcare for children. Within a couple of years, the party's popularity was sky-high and talking about bringing the region closer to the center made no sense. Awolowo used the popularity of the party, to depose the Alaafin, an act that would have been considered sacrilegious at any other time, but which passed without much of a whimper from the public, due to the popularity of the party. This did not end the problems within the party though.

As the legal adviser of the party, Akintola certainly knew about the resistance of the likes of Awolowo and Enahoro to the British push for an alliance between the Action Group and the NPC. So, Akintola's continued dalliance with Ahmadu Bello was nothing short of defiance to, and open rebellion against his own party's leadership, agenda and philosophy. Perhaps the English Colonials had something on him, or he was just carrying a moral burden to pay for his scholarship.

Despite all this, Awolowo decided to give up the premiership of the Western Region to serve as the leader of the opposition after the 1959 elections. It was a curious decision that may have proven very costly for the emerging Nigerian nation. Despite the clear unpopularity of this move, Akintola's open romance with the Fulbe NPC leader, Bello continued. It got to a head when he was absent from his own party's convention in 1962; instead, he was with Ahmadu Bello at the University of Ibadan commissioning a hall in honor of Muhammed Bello, the second Fulbe ruler of Hausaland, slave raider of millions of indigenous peoples, and the younger Bello's progenitor.

This provocation led to the removal of Akintola as the deputy leader of the party, which automatically meant impeachment from his position as the Premier of the Western Region. Ahmadu Bello quickly expressed a very strong and public support for Akintola.

There was a very minor fracas that was limited to about five NCNC members in the Western region legislative house when it was time to ratify Akintola's removal as premier. These four or five NCNC supporters of Akintola in the 80-member house tried to disrupt proceedings by seizing the mace, and based on that, the NPC-led federal government unbelievably declared a state of emergency in the Western region. This definitely had Ahmadu Bello written all over it, and sadly despite constant complaints about the excesses of his party leader, Prime Minister Tafawa-Balewa once again allowed himself to be a pass-through and failed to show independent leadership at this extremely pivotal point in Nigeria's steady descent to chaos.

Later in 1963, with Akintola reinstalled as Premier, the entire Action Group leadership was rounded up and tried, alongside their strategic allies such as Joseph Tarka of the United Middle Belt Congress. Anthony Enahoro was able to escape to Ghana and then England but eventually, despite some controversy, he was extradited to Nigeria to face trial and jailed along with most of the leadership of the Action Group.

L: Chief Anthony Enahoro back home for trial C: Enahoro in English police custody R: A young Abraham Adesanya was on the legal team fighting against the extradition of Enahoro

The NPC-led federal government eventually reinstalled Akintola to the Premiership of the Western Region despite the Action Group's election of Dauda Adegbenro as his replacement.

Even with significant external support and almost all the leadership of the Action Group behind bars, Akintola did not get the support and popularity from the public that he wanted, and maybe even craved. The 1965 elections that he contested were so significantly rigged that the head of the electoral commission refused to declare him as Premier and rather resigned from office. Adegbenro and the Action Group declared themselves as winners and the crisis in the Western Region, alongside other controversies going on with Zik and Balewa in the NCNC-NPC governing coalition in the Central Government (which included both men trying to assert control over the Military), led to the environments in which the military coups of 1966 and the Nigeria - Biafra War from 1967 occurred.

1966 Coups – Descent to Chaos

The Emmanuel Ifeajuna led coup of January 1966, and the Murtala Mohammed led attempt to divide the Nigerian State in July 1966, have been the subject of much discourse since then, with the former getting a larger share of the blame for triggering the subsequent civil war and other major problems Nigeria has faced since then, than the latter, whose counter-actions led to hostilities that included a brutal slaughter of almost 300 non-political regular officers and soldiers and thousands of civilians.

Considering the short and straightforward history of the Nigerian State, isolating the events of 1966 amounts to an attempt to avoid the obvious.

The very problem of Nigeria is Nigeria. The nation was set up by foreigners, for the benefit of foreigners and for the plundering of the local countries without the consent or input of the local peoples. That is the core essence and raison d'etre of the Nation and can almost certainly not be changed.

This fundamental deformity and flaw is forcefully suppressed, but never addressed, and those in control of the State pretend the foundational deficiencies don't exist and make vain but costly efforts to extinguish the ability of the (wholly or partly) constituent countries in the Nigerian State to function and progress. Little wonder that the Nigerian State has become the world's poverty capital, has the most out of school children, and is one of the worst places to live. The foreigners who are there to plunder, keep doing so aggressively, with a zombie-focused determination to feed on the corpse of the Nigerian nation, and its indigenous countries, if necessary.

One cannot help but see the obvious disconnect, especially since the indigenous countries and ethnicities have so much going for them in terms of resources, culture, and hardworking and enterprising people, and have always been sustainable. The problem with Nigeria is and has always been Nigeria.

The first two military coups will be examined as one continuous event, even though discussing the events of July 1966 with the required detail is usually not done, perhaps because many of those mutineers and mass murderers ended up being the rulers and shapers of the Nigerian state that emerged over the next half century.

No one is known to have been officially reprimanded, detained, interrogated or punished for sponsoring or executing the events of July 1966.

Most of the conspirators of the January 1966 attempt, though not yet officially punished, died shortly afterwards.

There is some pretty solid evidence that Nigeria's first President, Dr. Azikiwe, either bluffed about a coup, or was approached about one, as the crisis in the NPC-NCNC ruling coalition got worse in 1965. Given Zik's tendencies, he may have been bluffing, but there seems to be evidence of discussions of a coup with Ojukwu, who then tried to bring Yakubu Gowon, David Ejoor and Victor Banjo on board. Gowon and Ejoor outrightly rejected the idea[23], but Banjo didn't, and was reportedly open to an Ojukwu plan as long as it had a national base (presumably meaning that Gowon and Ejoor had to be on board as well). That doublemindedness, and openness to go along with Ojukwu was a mark of Banjo's tragic appearance on the stage of Nigerian history.

The fact that Lt. Col. Odumegwu Ojukwu theorized or advised against a coup that was perceived to be ethnically biased gave the impression that he might have been aware that the Ifeajuna plan was in the works.

While Azikiwe and Tafawa Balewa clashed over censuses, elections, election do-overs, and who had control of the military, Major Emmanuel Ifeajuna, Nigeria's first Commonwealth gold medalist, had started making plans for a coup. Ifeajuna was at the center of at least two groups with interests or roles in the coup, or to whom notification was given about the coup.

His fellow conspiring junior officers believed they were trying to instigate a revolution against the political class and the senior officers. On the other side, it seemed, were Zik and Aguiyi-Ironsi, who possibly individually sanctioned the coup or, at the very least, been notified ahead of the events. Like Murtala Muhammed would react to Yar'Adua a decade later, both Zik and Aguiyi-Ironsi may have given the impression that "well, I am [24]not against it, but don't mention my name if you get caught, and we'll do everything to save you." That was probably their stance towards the planned coup.

Ahead of the coup, Zik departed Nigeria on a medical vacation, again there was a parallel to the actions of Murtala Muhammed a decade later, who also, somehow, was outside the country while Shehu Musa Yar'Adua plotted Yakubu Gowon's removal. Zik's personal Doctor who accompanied him on the trip, eventually abandoned him abroad in December 1965, when he could not figure out the need to extend the trip.

That first coup eventually occurred on January 15, 1966, with Kaduna, Ibadan, and Lagos as the primary action points. Prime Minister Abubaker Tafawa-Balewa, Finance Minister Festus Okotie-Eboh, Northern Region Premier Ahmadu Bello, and his wife Hafsatu, Brigadier Ademulegun and his wife Latifat, Brigadier Maimalari, Colonel Shodiende, Colonel Kur Mohammed and Lt. Cols Unegbe, Pam and Lagerma were among the leading politicians and senior military officers murdered by the Coup plotters. About 10 other civilians and military officers were also killed during the Coup. The killing of Lt. Col Unegbe, a senior Military supply Officer, with no key command or control over troops, but significantly the only Igbo officer killed, only seemed to raise suspicion of a senseless murder done to give the impression of non-ethnic agenda[25].

*L: **Brigadier Maimalari** R: **Brigadier Ademulegun:** Maimalari was Nigeria's first Regular Officer. Not promoted from the NCO ranks, or with a Short Service Commission, or a Subaltern or other contract training arrangement.*

At the time, Major Olusegun Obasanjo had just returned to Kaduna on a course and was staying with Major Nzeogwu; he did not play any role in the coup. However, another officer who had recently returned from an overseas course, Yakubu Gowon, would play a crucial role in suppressing the coup. Indeed, he was one of the few shining lights amidst the tragedies of both military coups. Other significant participants in stopping the coup, or limiting the carnage were Lt. Col. David Ejoor and RSM Tayo of Bonny Camp.

David Ejoor was the commander at Enugu; he happened to be in Lagos at the time. According to reports, he either unilaterally arrested the convoy coming from Abeokuta or at least decoyed the group towards their arrest/surrender. Then he returned to Enugu to check the situation at his base.

It was RSM Tayo of Bonny camp who, realizing that something was amiss, locked the armory and had all the NCOs left in the barracks to sit in the open field. Since there was no information on who was attacking or what side was planning the coup, he took the measure to forestall violent incidents out of irrational fear.

The principal executors of the coup were Nzeogwu in Kaduna, Nwobosi in Ibadan, Ifeajuna, and others, including Ademoyega in Lagos. Nwobosi arrested the deputy Western premier Remi Fani-Kayode in Ibadan and brought him to Lagos, where he (Fani-Kayode) was eventually released by

Gowon and reportedly taken away by Victor Banjo afterwards.

Even to the most liberal mind, General Aguiyi-Ironsi's actions relating to the coup gave room to doubt that he was ignorant of the events that unfolded on that day. First, he supposedly received a phone call from Lt. Col James Pam, informing him of the coup, around 3 am on the morning of the coup. Pam, however, did not live to give an independent corroboration of this fact. Ademoyega had led a team to disconnect the manual Lagos telephone switch around this time. Several key personalities, including the British high commissioner, could not use their phones that morning, but Aguiyi-Ironsi credits this call for keeping him ahead of the situation.

Aguiyi-Ironsi claimed to have intimidated the boys on Carter Bridge led by Captain Orji to cross over from Lagos Island to the Mainland on his way to Ikeja Cantonment. This was strange given the violence perpetrated by the plotters a few hours before. Aguiyi-Ironsi eventually made it to the military cantonment in Ikeja on the mainland of Lagos, close to the airport. It seemed he and the commander just got the officers together and waited without any specific action being taken. Gowon, who was the incoming commander of the base and had just returned from a lieutenant colonel's course in the UK a few days earlier, was the one who mobilized a quick reaction force to the island of Lagos, where all the government offices and key leaders of the country resided. Gowon's quick reaction force included a certain Lieutenant Muhammadu Buhari, and the team was able to check on all the key senior officers and get a real-time assessment of who was missing. They also arrested a couple of the plotters and executioners.

In the early morning hours following the coup, it became apparent that the Prime Minister was missing. The most senior NPC minister, Inuwa Wada, was in Europe for medical treatment as the coup played out, leaving Bukar Dipcharima, a former Zikist who was previously in the NYM and NCNC as the most senior NPC politician in the cabinet. He had approached the British High Commissioner Francis Cumming-Bruce for possible military assistance, but it seems Cumming-Bruce, after consulting with some other British officials locally, decided to sit back and see which side emerged victorious from the situation and support whoever won the control of the Nigerian State.

As previously mentioned, English interests in Nigeria after the Second World War centered around having access to Nigerian, especially Hausa troops to fight and die for the English cause if necessary. There was therefore no appeal to having English soldiers come to die for and in a Nigeria that had lost its strategic importance. This was just before the emergence of Crude Oil as a major strategic interest.

In any case, the Senate President Nwafor Orizu, as Acting President (in Nnamdi Azikiwe's absence), refused to swear Dipcharima in as the interim Prime Minister. The NCNC ministers insisted that Dr. Ozumba Mbadiwe was the most senior cabinet minister and should be the acting Prime Minister instead. However, the NPC insisted on Dipcharima. It was important to have an Acting Prime Minister, because the British High Commissioner maintained that a request for military assistance had to be channeled appropriately through a serving or acting Prime Minister. Nevertheless, it didn't seem that the British were going to grant that request anyway.

Perhaps disgusted by the inability of the politicians to choose an acting Prime Minister or just trying to seize the chance to rule the country, Aguiyi-Ironsi had a meeting with his junior officers, supposedly trying to get the support of the military to take over. Gowon, again, was a strong voice in opposition to the military getting involved in civilian rule. Aguiyi-Ironsi also met with a gathering of the remnants of the government comprising cabinet members and other senior politicians. However, he supposedly called Orizu aside for a private meeting; once Orizu came out of the meeting, he declared that he would not swear in Dipcharima as acting Prime Minister. Eventually, the politicians yielded power to Major General Aguiyi-Ironsi as the civilian cabinet members were forced to read a prepared speech with gun-toting soldiers on standby. Cabinet members reported that he also gave them the 'You either hand over as Gentlemen, or you hand over by Force' option.

That was a major mistake on the part of Aguiyi-Ironsi, and the allure of power may have shielded him from the reality that a direct Military Government, especially under these circumstances was only going to increase the instability inherited from the political process, and not quell it, especially if he was going to be under any constraint, time or otherwise, regarding the quick trial of the January 15 plotters.

David Ejoor, possibly one of two officers leading efforts to actively investigate and suppress the coup, gave a troubling account of Aguiyi-Ironsi in Ikeja, pistol drawn, and asked him, David, are you with me or against me?

Victor Banjo's again made a puzzling and eventually ill-advised decision, as he was quickly arrested afterwards during a visit to Aguiyi-Ironsi's office, where he had suggested that he was ready to help the government. He may have been trying to gain some leverage on his wavering 'yes' to Ojukwu's request a few months earlier, but as these things play out, there is never enough room at the top and the Governorship of the Western region (which would have matched Banjo's 'rank and profile') was already penned down for Adekunle Fajuyi, who was sympathetic to the Ifeajuna coup.

Aguiyi-Ironsi's best option was probably not to accept or take over power in the first place, but once he was in power by happenstance, opportunity or design, his best option at survival and stability in the country, outside of a quick trial of the coupists, would have been to separate the military along regional lines, and quickly tried to solidify federalism or aim for a loose confederation. That would have diffused the tension to a large extent and communicated that there was no plan of domination by one group or ethnicity over the rest of the country or another.

The fact that there were real imbalances in the numbers (Hausas dominated NCO rank and file for instance) would not have been a problem if a regional Government was increasing the numbers for its regional Army. The Bello-Ribadu policy would have been no problem for a regional Military.

Rather, Ironsi seemed to pursue a Unification approach and appointed a Commissioner for an Administration for a Unified Nigeria, while abolishing the Hausa language requirement for the Northern Civil Service. This, along with a speech by the Eastern Military Governor, Lt. Col Ojukwu that Eastern Civil Servants could be transferred to other regions based on seniority only increased fears, especially in the far North that the January 1966 coup was a means for subjugation.

Aguiyi-Ironsi also delayed the trial of the coup plotters. Some have suggested that he was afraid of putting Ifeajuna on trial. This was highly suspicious, especially since other separatists who were not coup plotters like Isaac Adaka Boro and his Niger Delta Volunteer Force colleagues had been arrested, tried and sentenced in that same period. It was indeed curious that Aguiyi-Ironsi, who had lost two of his Brigadiers, and had claimed to be top of the elimination list of the January plotters, was viewed as being personally responsible for delaying the trial of the coup plotters. Ademoyega wrote about Ifreajuna's opposition to having him handle this critical part (eliminating Ironsi) of their plot, and assigning him to the telephone disconnection, and other assignments on the day.

In addition to Aguiyi-Ironsi's strategic and governance errors, there were other basic tactical and operational mistakes that also led to his death in July 1966.

The plotters of July '66 knew that Lagos was Aguiyi-Ironsi's stronghold and that an attack there was likely to meet a lot of opposition. So, they had planned to carry out the coup outside of Lagos. It was an operational failure therefore, that there was no immediate evacuation plan (perhaps with a chopper) in place for the Head of State in Ibadan and for his shuttles to places outside of Lagos. Ironsi requested for a helicopter, which arrived after he and Fajuyi had been led away. In any case, it could be argued that a chopper would have been an easy target with the building already surrounded. It might have been a deterrent, if already part of the Head of State's entourage though.

After the first coup, especially with the delay in trying the detained coupists, Lt. Col. Murtala Muhammed started coordinating action for a countercoup, setting a date for July 29. He called off this initial date, fearing that his plot had been discovered when he was confronted by an intelligence officer, Lt. Col. Patrick Anwunah, who said he knew the plan was to kick off that night. Anwunah notified a couple of commanders, including the garrison commander in Abeokuta, Lt. Col. Okonweze. The latter gathered all the officers in his unit together in the mess and tried to appeal for calm and reason to prevent any bloodshed.

This peace meeting, however, in a counter-productive fashion, triggered the July 1966 coup. One of the NCOs assumed that there were plots to eliminate Northern soldiers. This lone NCO rallied his colleagues, and the Armourer, who issued weapons to northern NCOs. These NCOs promptly went into the meeting conveyed by their Commander and killed him, and other officers of Igbo origin.

It didn't help that Lieutenant Mwadkon Pam, the younger brother of Lt. Col. James Pam, who was killed in January '66, was serving in Abeokuta and was out for revenge. Okonweze had planned to take all soldiers to the Armory to pick up arms and ammunition so they could defend themselves. A radically different strategy to that taken by the Warrant Officer in Bonny Camp six months earlier There is no guarantee of success by either one of these strategies, however. The Okonweze strategy of issuing weapons to everyone to act as a deterrent, was successful in Enugu, for instance.

Following the killings in Abeokuta, Lt. Mwadkon Pam placed a call to Lt. Garba Dada to inform him that 'Aure

Paiko' was in full gear. Dada then rallied the conspiring Soldiers of the 4th battalion in Ibadan (seen as one of the successor Divisions of the 'Glover's Hausa's, the Army's founding unit), woke the visiting Major Theophilus Danjuma, who was on the entourage of the Head of State, but was staying in the barracks.

Operation Araba/Aure Paiko

When the mutineers in Abeokuta contacted Murtala Mohammed, it reportedly had a domino effect on most or all the other army formations, with the feeling that failure to follow through would leave the guys in Abeokuta exposed. Secondly, failing to arrest the head of state, Aguiyi-Ironsi, would also make the effort fruitless. With Murtala Muhammed as the unofficial command center, the killings started at different military formations.

For most Nigerians born in the 70s and 80s, the official accounts and records of contemporary Nigerian history, especially the events of the 1960's and 1970's are scant and essentially useless.

There are however pointers and indicators that force an extremely positive bias or impression or some of the actors and participants in the major events, and perhaps no one is a bigger beneficiary of this, than Murtala Ramat Muhammad, His face adorned the 20 naira note, the highest local currency (fiat money) available at the time and for a couple of decades. His name adorned the leading international airport in the country, and he is meant to occupy an exalted status in the minds and lives of Nigerians, a combination of Kennedy, Eisenhower, Roosevelt, and General Douglas MacArthur all rolled into one.

Sir Ahmadu Bello, with his Officers at Mons.

Many Nigerian kids at the time grew up knowing the rhyme describing the wife of Buka Suka Dimka, who was accused of killing Murtala Muhammed. It was something along the lines of, "Dimka's wife, what are you doing in the market, Shame (on you); Go home because Dimka is about to be killed." So, as a child growing up then, in your mind or your subconscious, Murtala Mohammed occupied a saintly, sacred role that should not be questioned.

The reality is not quite straightforward. Murtala Mohammed may have had a change of heart as he became the head of state, primarily due to the events that led to his assumption of the position, which occurred about a decade after the current reference point. However, the pre-1975 Murtala fell far short of the image presented by the scant official records and propaganda.

The entire July Coup/Partition attempt was nicknamed *Aure Paiko* or 'Paiko's wedding.' 'Paiko' was the nickname of Lieutenant Garba Dada, the Adjutant of the fourth battalion in Ibadan, Perhaps Dada was to get married around the time of the coup, which would provide a cover for the plotters if heard discussing the upcoming 'wedding' in Ibadan.

Captains Bali and Remawa in Abeokuta were the first to notify the Army headquarters of the killings. Both were out of the barracks on a night out to town and thus were not part of the action, but when they got back to base, they saw the dead bodies and got in touch with Army HQ in Lagos.

Lt. Col. Gowon, now the Army Chief of Staff, had to worry about suppressing a rebellion for the second time in six months. This time, he faced a formidable opponent in Murtala Muhammed, who had the backing of the majority of the Hausa and other Northern NCOs of the Army and the entire Bello-Ribadu Officer Corps, which was now a significant portion, if not the majority of Junior Officers (the Second Lieutenants, and Lieutenant especially) of the Army.

It appears that by 3 am, soldiers from the 4th battalion led by Lieutenant James Onoja with Major Danjuma in tow, had cordoned off the Governor's Residence, where the Head of State was staying. Other officers, including Lt. Shelleng, and Lt. Dada (Paiko) took some soldiers from the group of about 30 on assignments, including mounting checkpoints to neutralize any incoming troops from Lagos, or Abeokuta (both less than 100 miles to the South of Ibadan).

However, Aguiyi-Ironsi was not arrested until after 8 am. This may have been due to Danjuma trying to buy time, as he was essentially an 'outsider' now leading an operation in

Ibadan. He stalled attempts to blow up the building, perhaps believing that it was better to have the Head of State alive as a negotiation tool if necessary, but things escalated when the commander of the 2nd division (Ikeja Cantonment) in Lagos, Lt. Col. Njoku, who was with the Head of State earlier in the night, but was staying in an adjoining Guest House, shot his way past the Soldiers surrounding the building. Onoja, afraid that Njoku was going to get help to crush the coup, escaped, leaving Danjuma at the head of troops who barely knew him, with some suspecting that he was a Hausa speaking Igbo. He was about to completely lose the weak hold he had on the situation.

That Danjuma's Jukun homeland was in the 'North was due to Lugard's fiscal and geographical gerrymandering but delving into that would be tangential to the matters at hand.

Shelleng's return eased the tension a bit, and a survey of the grounds, close to the Guest House where Njoku had escaped from led to a conversation between Gowon, now Army Chief of Staff, and Danjuma. Gowon and Ogundipe (Brigadier, Chief of Staff Supreme Headquarters) had tried to reach Ironsi and Fajuyi without success and called the Guest House). Gowon was able to confirm that Murtala (actually Lieutenants Pam and Paiko, but with Murtala's blessings) was ahead of him in Ibadan and appealed to Danjuma that there should be no bloodshed.

Ironsi and Fajuyi then sent Ironsi's Northern Army ADC Lt. Sanni Bello outside to investigate the situation, and he (Bello) was promptly detained by the Coupists. Ironsi's Southern Air Force ADC Lt. Andrew Nwankwo remained inside. Fajuyi then stepped outside to speak to Danjuma and the group and is followed inside by Danjuma and about five fully armed soldiers.

Once inside, Danjuma accuses Ironsi of organizing the killing of "brother-officers" in January and not bringing 'the so-called dissident elements' to justice, and recounted how he (Danjuma) had taken risks and run around to calm the ranks, but nothing had been done close to the end of July.

It is extremely important to note that the military officers (at least those who enlisted before the Bello-Ribadu Officers) were not as concerned about the death of the civilian politicians in January. The killing of military officers, who were not involved in governance of the country, broke a brotherhood bond, and pointed more fingers back to Ironsi. The killings of the Brigadiers and Colonels who may have challenged Ironsi's decision to 'accept the invitation of the civilian cabinet' to lead, was a bitter pill to swallow for many of the officers of the Army. All of this played out within a year of Ironsi gaining command of the Army as the GOC.

Danjuma and the arrested team then marched Ironsi, Fajuyi and Nwankwo out to join the detained Sanni Bello, and attempted to take them to a secure location, but Paiko, and the Ibadan team resisted the move, as their own instructions from Murtala had nothing to do with Danjuma's 'no bloodshed arrangement' with Gowon.

Meanwhile, Lt. Col Murtala Muhammed was going round the military formations in Lagos, waking the conspirators up and telling them to get ready for action. He was almost pre-empting and sometimes countering Gowon, the Army Chief of Staff who was trying to rally troops to restore order and resist and prevent the killings. The relationship between Murtala Muhammed and Gowon was to take this form over the next decade and even beyond. Gowon kept trying to exert authority in a sometimes-diplomatic way but remained quite conscious of Murtala Muhammed's popularity. However, Murtala Muhammed was always the subversive subordinate, having realized that he had 'street credibility' and could counter Gowon without consequence.

Murtala even wrote a letter to Gowon in the 70's, apologizing for all the times he had made life difficult for Gowon, despite his senior officer's effort to accommodate his excesses. Shortly afterwards, he (Murtala) sanctioned or organized the coup that removed Gowon from office as Head of State.

It is almost pointless listing out those involved in this mass murders of July 1966, as just about everyone you can imagine who has played a role in Nigeria since, including future Heads of State, participated in this orgy of killings. While the self-preservation argument has been pushed, especially once the killings in Abeokuta started, these killings were not in self-defense, as there was no clear and immediate threat to the lives of the perpetrators. More so, almost all the officers and men killed in the July 1966 Mass Murders had no business with the January 1966 Coup. The best some of the perpetrators of the murders could come up with was to accuse them of taunting. They claimed that Igbos were taking over, pointing to provocative songs and statements.

As has been pointed out and remains obvious, the basis for the creation of the Nigerian state was the plundering and parochial intentions of Europeans over a limited stretch of time. There is no real basis for the existence of the legal and fiscal unit that is the Nigerian State as structured post-colonially, though it is possible and even beneficial for the entrapped countries to negotiate an economic union or confederation in which the constituent countries will be separate fiscal and legal unit, in an economic union and with key Joint Administrative Areas.

This is probably the only way to curtail the inherent weaknesses and vices of the foreign created state, which continues to witness systemic and routine cycles of violence and corruption that drag the indigenous countries and peoples to lower levels of poverty, illiteracy, extremism, and other clear forms of retrogression.

Returning to Aure Paiko, there was action in all the other military formations and regional capitals, except maybe Benin City, although there were some initial signs of restraint and containment in Enugu and Kaduna, but this would not.

Captain Martin Adamu, a key conspirator loyal to Murtala, soon took over the intelligence center of the Army Headquarters. Brig. Ogundipe, Lt. Col. Gowon, Lt. Col Anwunah (Army Intelligence) and Maj. Mobolaji Johnson set up a rival decision-making operation center at the Police headquarters, similar to the strategy of the British police Assistant IGP Marsden and High commissioner Francis Cuming-Bruce, who, six months earlier, had used the police headquarters and its Independent communication capability since the public phone lines had been cut.

From Left to Right sitting: Captain Adeyinka Adebayo,Captain Philip Effiong,Captain Imo,Major Samuel Adesoji Ademulegun,Major Wellington Bassey,General Forster, Major JTU Ironsi,Major Ralph Shodeinde,Captain Zakaria Maimalari, Captain Conrad Nwawo, Captain David Ejoor.

Middle Row standing: Lt Igboba,Lt George Kurubo, (non Nigerian standing next to Kurubo), Lt J Akaga,Lt Patrick Anwunah, Lt Louis Ogbonnia, Lt Chukwuemeka Odumegwu Ojukwu, Lt Eyo Ekpo, Lt Arthur Unegbe, Lt Abogo Largema

Back Row: Lt Hilary Njoku, 2nd Lt Nzefili, 2nd Lt Ogunenwe, 2nd Lt Shadrak, Lt Madiebo,2nd Lt Anthony Eze, Lt Yakubu Gowon, 2nd Lt Sylvanus Nwanjei,Lt Yakubu Pam, 2nd Lt Hassan Katsina.

Those not in the picture are Captain Kur Mohammed,Lt Victor Banjo and Lt Michael Okwechime

1st generation of indigenous Nigerian Army Officer[26]

Murtala Muhammed must have figured that there could be no coming back from the madness playing out at different formations all over the country. The plotters had appointed a certain Sergeant Dickson to secure the airport and commandeer a couple of planes that would fly the northern rebelling soldiers and their families out of Lagos to Kano once the Aure Paiko was done. There was no way anyone could get away with all the killings and carnage. Nigeria had been partitioned, and there was a speech ready for the announcement.

Ogundipe and Gowon rolled the dice and put out a quick reaction force to take control of the airport, but soldiers waylaid them at Ikeja. And in the shoot-out that ensued, about 30 soldiers were reportedly killed and sadly, some civilians, including some expatriates, such as the head of a major shoe company at the time. That was the end to any real opposition to the rebellion. It was now down to the inevitable partitioning and maybe appeals and negotiation.

Nigeria was in a fluid state on Friday, July 29, and Saturday, July 30, 1966. The soldiers led by Murtala Mohammed had mostly achieved their killing and carnage objective in most parts of the country and wanted to proceed with their partitioning of the country, but other than demands for everyone to return to their regions, they clearly had no clue how to get this done. They were the ones with the guns though, and in Nigeria, which has mostly been sufficient.

There were a couple of interesting (if that word could be used for such tragic events) bylines to the crazy killing orgies of this period. A second (compromised) quick response team was dispatched by Ogundipe and Gowon, under the command of a Second Lieutenant Usman or Osuma. He had probably joined the army courtesy of his Hausa-speaking abilities and due to the Bello-Ribadu policy, but he was actually from the East; there were many others like him in the Army. 'Usman,' like Onoja in Ibadan, skipped out of town, leaving all the craziness behind, with his life intact.

The military governor of the East, Lt. Col. Ojukwu, took preemptive action and left Enugu for Onitsha, probably because he was unsure of what was going on and maybe felt comfortable around his family business' operational transfer base. Or perhaps he wanted to mobilize personal security. After all, in the First Republic, Shehu Shagari admitted to having hundreds of thugs armed with weapons in Obalende and other parts of Lagos just in case a struggle ever broke out. However, they were not particularly useful to Shagari or the NPC when trouble did eventually break out in January 1966, similar to the legion of Fani-Kayode's thugs in Ibadan.

Ojukwu resurfaced in Enugu and mirrored the situation in Lagos by using the police headquarters as a base instead of the military barracks. This decision could be explained by the fact that he was the military administrator (Governor) of the Eastern Region and not the commander of the Military base or troops.

Murtala Muhammed had contacted Lieutenant Yar'Adua to break into the armory, but the commander Lt. Col. Ogunnewe was able to take preemptive action that prevented the breakout of violence. Interestingly, the same approach had been attempted by Okonweze in Abeokuta but with very tragic consequences.

Ogunnewe managed to have a mixed group secure and guard the armory and de-armed everyone else except himself and had all the officers at the officers' mess and all the soldiers on the parade ground, all watching each other in a chilling stalemate. This was a better solution than the Mexican Stand-off Okonweze was said to propose in Abeokuta.

With the military checkmating itself in Enugu and Ojukwu in the safety of the Police Headquarters, He (Ojukwu) then started making demands of Lagos, especially Gowon and Ogundipe, who already had their hands very full with Murtala Mohammed, and the rampaging bulk of the rank and file of the Army.

In Kano, Lt. Col. Shuwa and Major Oluleye tried to maintain order to ensure that the ongoing chaos in Lagos and Ibadan did not spread there. The armory was secured before rampaging soldiers could get their hands on weapons. But some soldiers and civilians were killed anyway, and things got worse a few days later as civilians at the Kano airport trying to get out of town were killed by some NCOs, determined to join the orgy. Things soon got out of control, and Shuwa's attempt to get some Igbo Soldiers out of town ended badly with the execution of the soldiers by those meant to protect them. Shuwa soon had to escape from his own soldiers.

Shuwa, with Gowon

Part of the reason for the anger of the Northern NCOs in Kano was rumors about Igbo Officers stockpiling private weapons. Searches by Shuwa and Oluleye, perhaps meant to dispel the rumors and diffuse tension, however found the rumored private weapons.

Rather than this being proof of something sinister, the orgy of killings all over the country gave credence to the need for self-defense.

This captures the tragedy of the Nigerian State to a large extent. The indigenous countries and people, dealing with a forced and inefficient facade of unity in one conjoined state, spend more time worrying about defending themselves from attacks by other groups within and from outside the Nigerian State, than building prosperous and sustainable countries and societies. In many cases, the ability of these natural countries to exist, and perform is removed or suppressed.

In Kaduna, the Commander Lt. Col. Wellington Bassey was on leave, and his 2IC, Lt. Col Philip Effiong was out on Official Assignment. Lt. Col Alexander Madiebo, arrived from his Lagos base that morning, just making it out of the Lagos Airport before Murtala's killing posse seized the Airport. Sensing looming trouble, Madiebo was able to gather some Southern Lt. Cols and Majors to take preventive steps, so that when the killings started that night, a number of these officers were able to escape from Kaduna.

Many Officers were however still killed in gory manners by Bello-Ribadu Officers and NCOs. Some were however able to escape, due to the plans made earlier in the day, and the assistance from the Northern military Governor, Lt. Col. Hassan Katsina.

Major Obasanjo, for instance, was reportedly smuggled out of town, in the boot of a car to Maiduguri. Lt. Col. Hassan Katsina provided Major Ogbemudia with a land rover jeep to facilitate his escape.

Major Ogbemudia had detained Lt. Dimka a few days earlier as he (Dimka) tried to break into the armory. Perhaps Dimka was trying to be the one to set things off, to impress Lt. Col Murtala Muhammad, the Chief Plotter and Commander of Aure Paiko. Dimka was released to de-escalate the growing tension, but he had marked Ogbemudia for termination.

Upon learning of Ogbemudia skipping town, he organized a chasing gang of soldiers determined to kill the man that had detained him a few days earlier. Ogbemudia, refueled and may have stopped a bit at a catering rest stop a few hundred miles outside Kaduna, unaware of this pursuit. This gave Dimka and the chasing party the opportunity to catch up, and the chasing and shooting reportedly continued all the way to Owo, over 500 kilometers away from Kaduna, where Ogbemudia, running out of fuel, abandoned the jeep, dashed into the bush, and was able to escape his determined hunters.

Frontpage announcement of the capture of Lt. Col B.S Dimka after a Nationwide manhunt for the killing of Head of State, Gen. Murtala Muhammad. Less than a decade earlier, Dimka was the hunter in a literal cross-country manhunt, determined to kill, as part of a conspiracy to divide the country led by the then Lt. Col Murtala Muhammad.

Just under a decade later, Lt. Col Buka Suka Dimka ironically and symbolically turned his guns on General Ramat Murtala Muhammad, the Head of the Nigerian State, with these words,

"Good morning fellow Nigerians, This is Lt. Col. B. Dimka of the Nigerian Army calling. I bring you good tidings. Murtala Muhammed's deficiency has been detected. His government is now overthrown by the young revolutionaries."

Lt. Col. Ogunnewe's commendable efforts at maintaining the peace in Enugu were among the more impressive efforts along with those of Hassan Katsina and Shuwa at a time of complete chaos and killings.

Things settled down a bit over the next few days, and the negotiations and power play started. It was decided that non-Eastern soldiers will leave the East and Eastern soldiers and civilians in other regions be allowed to come back to the East.

Sadly, in another telltale sign of a young army with poor planning, strategy, and execution, it appears the same train was meant to make an Enugu-Kaduna-Lagos-Enugu loop. This meant Eastern and Northern Soldiers on the same train on sections of this loop.

Major Adekunle was meant to accompany the Northern soldiers from the East to Kaduna and the Igbo soldiers from Kaduna back to the East.

Yar'Adua was said to be in the center of some action where some Igbo soldiers were killed and thrown off the train. This may have happened due to Yar'Adua wanting to gain some "credibility" following the peace that was maintained in Enugu, which showed a failure to achieve his instructions to gain control of the armory.

Adekunle's effort to intervene almost cost him his life, but for the intervention of Capt. Gibson Jalo.

Ultimately, this was a poor operation as there should never have been direct interaction of soldiers from different regions. Different trains or multiple trips could have been used to prevent such an incident. Good planning and strategy would have helped overcome limited time and resources.

This was, however, an Army that ultimately had no purpose, once its creators had left, and its objectives (British Interests and subjugation of the indigenous countries) had lapsed.

Nigeria's political leaders (the indigenous ones, especially) continue to follow the "Tafawa Balewa approach," which is a "balancing act of inefficiency," a haphazard approach of bringing everybody in and having up to 80 ministers. Development doesn't matter, corruption doesn't matter, just maintain some kind of balance and stability.

Yar'Adua's aggressive attempts to make up for his Enugu 'failure' in the following years did not impress some Bello-Ribadu officers but only brought more resentment. They were the ones who earned and restored the dominance of 'The North' with the killings of July 1966, but Yar'Adua was the one, getting double promoted from Lt. Col to Brigadier, and becoming the Deputy Head of State following Murtala's death.

It was therefore not surprising that despite having the most powerful political machinery in the Nigeria of the 1990's (the People's Democratic Movement, which says it is not a political party), Babangida, and later Abacha (reported to have additional 'personal beef' with Yar'Adua) always managed to cook up excuses to ban him from the political process.

They may not have been able to prevent his rapid and privileged rise in the Military, but they were going to prevent him from becoming Civilian President of the Nigerian State.

Shehu Musa Yar'Adua's younger brother, Umaru, succeeded Obasanjo as Nigeria's civilian President.

Tragically, the Nigerian Nation has little to do with the constituent countries or people but remains a balancing act of corruption, inefficiency, foreign interests, and violent propagation. No real progress or sustainable societies can be forged out of this.

A cursory observer would notice that the events of January and July 1966 largely (not completely) seemed to be a confrontation between the East and the North, even if a lot of the action was in Lagos, Ibadan and Abeokuta, within the 'Afeire' Confederacy.

It is worth noting that the Western region was massively underrepresented in the Officer Corps, but especially in the NCO ranks of the Nigerian Army. This was why there was no thought or mention of any Northern soldier leaving Lagos, Ibadan, Abeokuta, or even Benin (in the recently created Mid-West), as soldiers were asked to return to their regions. The West was essentially "occupied territory," without its own soldiers.

This was somewhat cultural and also due to the strategic or historical role that this part of the country has played. The Nigerian Army was not regarded as a noble or desirable position for the best and brightest from the region. It seemed like it was meant for those who were considered rascals and who, at least at the time, had no excellent career prospects. Interestingly, this strategy of 'recruiting from the streets' was what Benjamin Adekunle adopted, when asked to build the 43rd Marine Commando from the group up, during the Nigeria-Biafra War. Hence the unique constitution of the Glover's Hausas and Lagos Constabulary, as described earlier in this book.

It is also a window into the cautious and somewhat cagey nature with which that entire part of Nigeria, referred to here as Afeire Confederacy[27] has always viewed and continues to view the Nigerian experiment. While it hasn't violently resisted it, it has probably been most slowed and negatively impacted by the Nigerian State. They view political figures who try to drag them into an English or Fuduyan Fulbe-dominated center with grave suspicion, whether it was Akintola or Abiola or Obasanjo or even as of 2021, Tinubu. Yet, they have always reacted angrily if they felt any of these leaders, except Akintola, were mistreated, having ticked all the boxes. Most of the southwestern part of the country has always been occupied territory in essence, as far as the military was concerned.

This, put in context, made Ojukwu's demands on Ogundipe and Gowon in the reality of 'Aure Paiko' as nothing more than tantrums and mere wishes.

The Igbo dominance of the Officer Corps, and the historical dominance of the NCO ranks by Hausas and Hausa speaking soldiers from the proposed 'Central Region' pre-amalgamation (currently known as the middle belt), was the picture of the Army that Ahmadu Bello, and Ribadu desperately tried to alter. Prime Minister Tafawa Balewa seemed relaxed in the fact that the 'man behind the rifle' was Hausa, or

Hausa speaking, and did not want to lower standards for the Officer Corps.

Another interesting side note from Lagos on July 29, was the young Captain Joseph Garba, who was very much part of the plots with Murtala Mohammed, but had with Paul Tarfa, heroically hidden Igbo colleagues at the National Guards Company (Brigade of Guards) in Ikoyi, on Lagos Island , as Abeokuta unexpectedly triggered 'Aure Paiko'.

Garba was called upon by Gowon and Ogundipe to try to quell the coup (that he was technically a part of), and was said to have made at least three trips between the Police headquarters on Lagos Island, where the loyal commanders were holed up, and the large 2nd Battalion in Ikeja (Maryland Cantonment) on the Mainland of Lagos where Murtala Muhammed was with, and had control of the bulk of the troops of the Army.

This would not be the last time that Joseph Garba would have to make runs back and forth and try to split the difference between Murtala Mohammed and Yakubu Gowon.

Aure Paiko and the Nigerian State

Ibadan was suggested as an easy location to arrest the head of state because it was majorly made up of a large contingent of Hausa northern soldiers, who were seething from anger that three former Northern commanders of the local fourth division (Maimailari, Kur Muhammed, and Largema), were killed in the January 1966 coup. The fact that the plotters had not been court-martialed or tried not only solidified the belief of Ironsi being the invisible hand behind Ifeajuna, but fueled rumors that the plotters could be released once Ironsi had significantly consolidated power.

There were riots in May 1966 following the unitary government declaration of Aguiyi-Ironsi that created 35 "provinces of regions." The Nigerian government today, though masked as a federal republic, is still effectively *that* unitary state. These riots were in Kano, Bauchi, Katsina, Zaria, Sokoto between May 4th and 5th, and they left about 600 Igbo civilians dead. That was a vital sign that the anger in the core Fulbe-controlled Hausa heartland was not just in the Army but also on the streets, spearheaded by the religious institutions and societal leaders.

It is interesting to note that this was only in the core Fulbe-controlled Hausa heartland. There were no riots in Borno, Ilorin, Makurdi, Igala land and other areas. This fact naturally indicates the different constructs of various parts of the gerrymandered North, a fact that official propaganda aggressively denied.

Aure Paiko eventually kicked off as Lieutenant Mwadkon Pam, or people close to him, ignored Murtala's order to delay the coup. The younger Pam was determined to avenge the killing of his older brother, Lt. Col James Pam, in January. Pam contacted Paiko (Garba Dada), and they got in touch with Murtala Muhammed, who would after deliberating a bit and realizing that things had already kicked off at Abeokuta, authorized the action in Ibadan.

It's never easy or accurate to draw stereotypes out of difficult situations and events. Still, if one could create a stereotype of the Nigerian Army before independence, it would be one of Igbo Officers commanding Hausa Soldiers.

When told by his own inspector-general of police that Easterners (technically ethnic Igbo Mid-Westerners, but this is a bit of Nigerian *ITK*) led most of the key strategic and combat positions in the Nigerian army, Prime Minister Tafawa Balewa replied that he was well aware of this, but that *'the man behind the rifle is a northerner.'* This was also why Muhammadu Ribadu and Ahmadu Bello made a case to the Prime Minister, shortly after independence, for the mass entrance of Northern soldiers to the officer cadre. The stereotype was certainly not imaginary.

This was also why as the demand by Afeire leaders for the withdrawal of 'Northern' troops from their region[28] was completely ignored even as military personnel from the East returned to their region, and those from other regions left the East. The Western region did not have significant numbers in the Officer Corps and the Non-Commission cadre of the military. The reported role of Olusegun Obasanjo in neutralizing attempts to demand for the departure of Northern troops from the Western region gives an insight to why he remained unpopular in his 'home' region for several decades, and almost always lost elections there, after his post-prison transition to politics. Such move, if effected, may have prevented the War and set Nigeria solidly on a path of a healthy confederacy.

It almost seems futile talking about heroes in such an orgy of bloodletting as *Aure Paiko* which was accompanied by the killings of tens of thousands of civilians afterwards.

It is, however, impossible to take a critical look at the first two coups d'etat and not commend Yakubu Gowon's role. He was indeed Army Chief of Staff when all hell broke loose, but he had distinguished himself at every point in that critical January to July 1966 period.

He firmly expressed the danger of Aguiyi-Ironsi taking power in January 1966. Even as the entire rank and file of the army were running rampant, he tried to counter, putting himself at significant risk, but maintaining the chain of command, deferring first to Aguiyi-Ironsi and subsequently to Ogundipe. Notwithstanding that, it was a considerable risk to counter a rampaging Murtala Muhammed who had pretty much partitioned the country since there was no coming back from the killings of hundreds of soldiers and tens of thousands of civilians that he and the others had triggered.

Other officers who were worthy of commendation include David Ejoor, especially for his actions in both Lagos and Enugu in January, as well as Lieutenant Colonels Alexander Madiebo and Hassan Katsina, and Major Ogbemudia for their efforts initially containing the spread of the orgy of killings to Kaduna. Be that as it may, they only had temporary success, and Hassan Katsina (with Major Abba Kyari) soon had to organize the escape of his fellow officers from Kaduna.

Lt. Col. Shuwa and Major Oluleye in Kano also deserve commendation, although their effort was only able to delay the bloodletting.

Lt. Col. Ogunnewe in the East, who maintained the previously mentioned mass stalemate.

Credit should be given to Lt. Col. Ojukwu as well. He withdrew from Enugu as the crisis started brewing, likely due to lack of information (you never know who is involved, and things would have been different if Yar'Adua gained access to the Armory), especially since he (Ojukwu) was a military governor and not necessarily an Army Commander at the time. His withdrawal to Onitsha, just 20 kilometers away from his Nnewi hometown, may have been to quickly mobilize independent logistics and security resources that were available due to his father's wealth. He was able to copy the command structure that was trying to hold the fort in Lagos as he operated from the police headquarters, independent of any compromised army command structure.

However, Ojukwu soon became a source of distraction to the effort to manage Lagos, probably allowing his rivalry with Gowon to fester unnecessarily. He seemed to irritate those in Lagos who already had to deal with Murtala Muhammed, even as the latter had the backing of most of the army's rank and file, including the junior Bello-Ribadu officers who were now dominant in the second lieutenant and lieutenant ranks and had the immediate and direct command of the troops. So, Ojukwu's insistence on maintaining the army's order was not just an irritation; it was almost plain stupidity at that point. Some writers and biographers, including Frederick Forsyth often ignore these facts in their account of events. Ojukwu's effort to recruit Gowon, Ejoor, and Banjo into the 'broad based' Azikiwe plot is also often missing. This plot, which eventually failed to take off, probably created the chasm between Ojukwu and Azikiwe on one hand, and Ojukwu and Gowon, on the other.

Other commendable acts of bravery during these days of madness include the actions of Lieutenant Sani Bello, who was joint ADC to the Head of State alongside Lieutenant Andrew Nwankwo. Bello and Nwankwo were being driven to what seemed like their deaths, along with Ironsi and Fajuyi.

Bello was however able to appeal to Dada (Paiko). They both hailed from the Minna-Kontagora axis on the southern fringes of Hausa land and the Northern area of Nupe country. Some other accounts suggested that Lt. Magoro caught up with the convoy, and had to plead for Bello's life. Bello then created a distraction, and based on a previously agreed signal, Nwankwo was able to escape into the bush. He then prevailed on the Soldiers not to go after him since he had achieved their objective in capturing Ironsi and Fajuyi.

Bello retired from the Army as a Colonel. As at 2021, he is one of Nigeria's wealthiest businessmen, an early investor in the largest telecommunications company in the country, the South Africa-owned MTN, and his son as of 2021, was the governor of his own Niger state, which is primarily Nupe country and the previously mentioned Kotangora and Minna divisions of Hausa land.

As for Paiko, the young adjutant in Ibadan whose nickname (and hometown) became the codename for the bloodbath for which no one was held accountable, not much is known about his subsequent military service or record. Nigerian Military blogger BEEGEAGLES, in reporting his death in 2020[29], said he was a Senator representing Niger State in the 2nd Republic (1979 - 1983).

Danjuma, like Joe Garba, would be caught between Murtala Mohammed and Yakubu Gowon. By his own admission, he had tried to quell growing resentment in the Army, in the hope that Ironsi would bring the January 1966 plotters to book, but his presence at the Governor's residence to arrest Ironsi and Fajuyi probably took a significant part of the fight out of Gowon, as Danjuma and Walbe would have probably been Gowon's first option to checkmate any moves Murtala was making in Ibadan.

His closeness to both officers (but particularly Gowon) probably cost him the opportunity of becoming the Head of the Nigerian State after Murtala Muhammed's assassination. As such, a compromise candidate was reached in the person of the highly reluctant, and some say terrified, Olusegun Obasanjo.

As the impact of Murtala Muhammed's decision to partition the country[30] and *Aure Paiko* began to unravel, the English represented by the British High Commissioner, the Super Perm Secs (as the core of about 3 to 5 permanent secretaries and civilian administrators were known), and Gowon took the central stage to reverse the partitioning of the Nigerian experiment.

The Perm Secs, The English Ambassador, and the American Ambassador were able to convince Murtala to reverse the already successful succession and partitioning, with the condition that the more stable Gowon became Head of State. Gowon, who had been arrested by Murtala and his mutineers upon his arrival in Ikeja, had a mini prisoner to palace story and emerged as Head of the Nigerian State.

It should be reiterated that it wasn't up to this 'kangaroo council' (describing it as anything but, would be a travesty) to determine the fate of naturally existing countries.

Murtala shows up in mufti (Civilian Clothing) to a Press Conference by the newly minted Major General Yakubu Gowon in 1968

The English would always act in their interest and so really cannot be faulted (but must be viewed with extreme suspicion and caution), after all, everyone has to do proper analysis and work for the best interest of their people. From the English perspective, Nigeria had moved from just another pawn in its competition with its European friends in the scramble for Africa, to a place to get soldiers to counter Germany in the first and second world wars. After the second world war, Hausa country, especially, became the most important piece to guarantee its insurance in the case of a third world war.

In the first military coup, England danced around the request for military assistance from Dipcharima, waiting to support whoever emerged victorious from the power play.

At the time, Nigeria was still important enough to be its fourth-largest embassy globally, and it even considered sending the Royal Prince down to Nigeria to be its ambassador. The events of 1966 made England step back a bit. Then, Araba/Aure Paiko made it seemed like power was swinging back to a Fulbe hegemony that had always danced to its (English or British, if you prefer) tune as a fellow foreign occupying power in the indigenous country of Hausas and, by extension Nigeria. The timing was key, as Crude Oil was beginning to play a more important role in global politics and economy. So, the English were only acting in their interests in keeping Nigeria together and supporting the North(ern Fuduyan Foreign Fulbe Hegemony).

Gowon, Ojukwu, Murtala and Awolowo

As previously mentioned, the central, even if unofficial narrative, in the Nigeria of the late 1970's and 1980's was to portray Gowon as the evil man that the villain Dimka was trying to bring back to power after the killing of Nigeria's saintly hero, Murtala Muhammed. The reality, however, doesn't match that narrative and perception. There was little in Gowon's career or character that suggested that he would have trusted the very unstable Dimka with such a task, even if he was behind a plot to unseat the Murtala Government.

Ojukwu, having to deal with the slaughter of hundreds of Igbo Officers and Soldiers and tens of thousands of Igbo civilians in various parts of the country, found Gowon's emergence as the Head of State unacceptable. It didn't help that he was also removed from Murtala Muhammad and the events in other parts of the Nigerian State.

Every statement or broadcast from Gowon seemed to be met by a counter statement or broadcast from Ojukwu. The bantering continued even up to counterclaims of each taking credit for the release of Obafemi Awolowo from the Calabar prisons.

In every way, Yakubu Gowon was a more moderate and restrained option than the Murtala of 1967, which makes it disappointing that an avoidable Civil War was not prevented.

A closer look at these four gentlemen in this crucial moment of Nigerian History is quite revealing.

Murtala, whose father was from Auchi, but landed in Kano via Agege, Lagos, was very much the arrowhead or Swordsman of the Foreign Fulbe controlled Hausaland. Ahmadu Bello promised to return to Lagos with a Sword. That promise was fulfilled by Murtala in the last days of July 1966.

He was very much the Military might in this situation, and represented the mindset of "domestic" colonials of Nigeria. This group has shown no real commitment to or interest in Nigeria, outside of control and plundering. It does not believe it is subject to the laws, and has no real interest in sacrificing for Nation-building. At this point, its objective was to get out of Nigeria as quickly as possible, as retaining control of Hausaland was better than an Igbo domination of a Unitary Nigeria.

Going back to 1966, the English Government, the senior Civil Servants (who can be viewed in some sense as successor to the Colonials) and Yakubu Gowon convinced Murtala and the Araba group to change its mind, since control over the 'subjugated south' as part of the whole country, was better than the 'Araba' that 'Aure Paiko' was meant to achieve.

Under the Buhari Administration from 2015 (or because of it, given Buhari's outlook and 'perspective') the Fuduyan Fulbes have actively collaborated with the (Nigerian) Kanuris in the control of the Nigerian State, following a century plus war in which the Fuduyan Fulbes failed to gain control of the religious and traditional institutions in Kanuri Country.

It must be pointed out that Murtala Muhammad showed signs of being a different person during his brief time as Head of the Nigerian State. He helped formulate a determined "Africa first," anti-Apartheid, non-aligned foreign policy for Nigeria, which was continued under Obasanjo, and saw Nigeria take aggressive steps to show its seriousness and commitment to this policy. This included the nationalization of British Petroleum, following the company's defiance of the instruction not to load Crude Oil from the Niger-Delta for the Apartheid South African Market and Government.

Maybe it was Murtala maturing, maybe it was just the initial 'gra-gra' of getting into office, maybe it was the rough reminder about his identity, following the difficult negotiations with military subordinates to ratify his selection as Head of State following the overthrow of Gowon by the Bello-Ribadu crew. He even made a trip to Auchi, and became particularly close to Ibrahim Kagara (Taiwo) for reasons that seem pretty obvious.

There was something different about the Murtala of 1975.

Gowon meets Awolowo upon his release from Prison, with Murtala watching closely

For the first seven months of 1966, **Lt. Col Yakubu Gowon** showed what was possibly the finest form of soldiering and military leadership that the Nigerian State had ever witnessed till that point, and possibly since. Gowon had been sterling, excellent and ultra professional, often swimming against the tide, occasionally walking on eggshells, trying to maintain what was sometimes a delicate balance, and at other times a raging inferno that could quickly turn around and consume him as well.

His actions as a Statesman did not meet the very high standards that he had set as a soldier over the previous 6 months; and he played a significant role as the English (represented by Francis Cumming-Bruce) and the Super Perm Secs' worked to reverse Murtala Muhammed's partitioning.

Gowon is Angas, whose home Country stretches from the Jos Plateau area to the current Federal Capital Territory in Abuja. Even though the Angas are indigenes of Jos, they are a minority of minorities, if that term can be used. When you think of Jos and Plateau, you think of the Beroms and the Taroks. And when you think of the FCT, you think of the Gbayis (or Gbagis) and the Nupes.

Gowon had to manage the Bello-Ribadu lieutenants and second lieutenants running amok with the largely Hausa-dominated (but with a significant number of middle-belt) NCOs in most of the Army formations in the previous days. His only shot at any relevance and probably survival lay in the united Nigerian state. In an Arewa Republic, or the Republic of Northern Nigeria, his position as a minority of minorities would be more than evident.

If he could barely contain Murtala Muhammed in the context of a political and military Nigeria, he would have no shot in the Republic of Northern Nigeria. As such, **G**o **O**n **W**ith **O**ne **N**igeria had as much to do with Gowon's survival and relevance as it did with keeping the English and Fuduyan Fulbe contraption together.

Thus, Gowon the soldier was excellent, Gowon the Statesman had his own biases, and some of these were self-preservatory. Given his ultra-minority profile, there was no way he was going to be a part of a Northern Arewa Republic with (or under the control of) Murtala Mohammed and the "out of control" Bello-Ribadu Lts and 2nd Lts.

From a military perspective, Western Nigeria was already occupied territory, given the history and development of the Nigerian Military (Glover's Hausas) up till that time. The region, a confederation of sub-ethnicities that were just rounding up their own internal civil wars (Ibadan had just negotiated a settlement with related Ekiti and Ijesha in the Kiriji war about the time the English Colonials were consolidating) and seemed ambivalent about a Nigerian State that had left almost a quarter of the country outside its borders.

The Action Group crisis, and the location of the 3 major military divisions (Lagos, Abeokuta and Ibadan) meant there was likely to be no problem from this region, despite a demand from its political leader for non-native soldiers to leave.

The Eastern region, even if not a subdued country, had just lost significant military manpower, and was definitely scarred by all the violence and killings that its people had suffered. It lacked the capacity to push back militarily at that time, especially in terms of personnel and to a large extent morale.

So, Nigeria made sense for Gowon, especially since he was now the negotiated choice to become the Head of State.

But, perhaps, his rational fear of the Arewa republic could have been placated with the middle-belt or central region within a Confederation of Nigerian States that gave each region the opportunity to live life and develop as it chose, but maintained the minimum terms of a Confederation agreement. Perhaps he had not seen the map on the cover of this book which predates Lugard's amalgamation or the replacing one Atahiru with another Atahiru in Sokoto. The map was a standard consideration for the Colonial Office, but was not the only one. Suggested territories and regions ranged from four upwards as realistic and individual subdivisions of a Nigerian Confederation that was definitely going to be Africa's most complex post-colonial state.

Obafemi Awolowo initially refused to join the fray, wanting to play the fatherly role of reconciling the young colonels and averting further disaster in the country. He even took a famous trip to Ojukwu in the East to try to mediate the crisis. However, as recounted in a couple of accounts, including Wole Soyinka's 'You Must Set Forth at Dawn', Ojukwu either reneged on an agreement or moved ahead of a deal that he should maintain the status quo for a couple of weeks (this was after the Aburi Accord) and not declare an independent republic.

Ojukwu seemingly countered this by suggesting that his last words to Awolowo was 'Baba, Atilo,' meaning "Old Man, we're already gone"

Awolowo was under pressure as a leader without troops. He had also previously turned down Gowon's request to join the government, even when Gowon asked Mrs. Awolowo to convince her husband[31]. However, he would eventually join the government of General Yakubu Gowon in a move that was not necessary, and maybe even ill-advised. It was excellent for the Nigerian State, but not for the sovereignty of the indigenous peoples and countries, which is what Awolowo had previously stood for, and resisted the British and Ahmadu Bello over in the 1950's. Over the next couple of years, he helped make the Nigerian State the strongest and most secure it had ever been.

A negotiated confederation would have been the best option for the Nigerian State at this critical time, and at every point in time since then. That was what the four main actors needed, without stating it, and for some, possibly without knowing it. This would have prevented the war, protected these leaders, and created the basis for long term growth and stability.

The inability of these men to achieve compromise and consensus, not necessarily Aburi, eventually led to the civil war; everyone acted in what they thought were their own short-term interests:

- It was in Gowon's interest for One Nigeria to continue, and as it was in the interest of the English.

- At this time, given what had occurred, it was probably in the interest of Ojukwu to form the Republic of Biafra even though most Ndi'Igbo take pride and speak about the uniting role they play in Nigeria through their commerce and migration.
- It is the interest of Fuduyan Fulbes (not Fulanis all over West Africa, but certainly the Fuduyan Fulbes rulers of Hausa Country) for Nigeria to continue existing.

A unitary or even federal Nigerian state was not in the interest of Awolowo or his people.

Awolowo may not have had an army to enforce political positions, and may have found it difficult to outrightly decline Gowon's invitation, but it might have been better for him to yield the position of deputy Head of Government position he had under Gowon to Enahoro or someone in his camp. He brought a few of his previously jailed comrades into the government, but his direct participation in the government gave Gowon the credibility to present the crisis as the Eastern region vs 'All of the rest of Nigeria.'

While Awolowo may have performed credibly well in the position, with the war financed without any debt and with relative fiscal discipline, his direct participation in the wartime government, and comments credited to him about starvation during a visit to parts of the Eastern region that had been captured by the Federal forces drew considerable criticism. In his own words,

'When I went, what did I see? I saw the kwashiorkor victims. If you see a kwashiorkor victim you'll never like war to be waged. Terrible sight, in Enugu, in Port Harcourt, not many in Cal-

abar, but mainly in Enugu and Port Harcourt. Then I enquired what happened to the food we were sending to the civilians. We were sending food through the Red cross, and CARITAS to them, but what happened was that the vehicles carrying the food were always ambushed by the soldiers. That's what I discovered, and the food would then be taken to the soldiers to feed them, and so they were able to continue to fight. And I said that was a very dangerous policy, we didn't intend the food for soldiers. But who will go behind the line to stop the soldiers from ambushing the vehicles that were carrying the food? And as long as soldiers were fed, the war will continue, and who'll continue to suffer? and those who didn't go to the place to see things as I did, you remember that all the big guns, all the soldiers in the Biafran army looked all well fed after the war, it is only the mass of the people that suffered kwashiorkor.

You won't hear of a single lawyer, a single doctor, a single architect, who suffered from kwashiorkor? None of their children either, so they waylaid the foods, they ambushed the vehicles and took the foods to their friends and to their collaborators and to their children and the masses were suffering. So I decided to stop sending the food there. In the process, the civilians would suffer, but the soldiers will suffer most.'

Awolowo voluntarily left the Government in 1971, shortly after the war. It can be argued that his participation in the war government was not in his interest, as he was now perceived as a willing participant in a brutal and avoidable war that he may have had enough influence to help prevent.

If there was anyone standing up for the victims of the mass killings of July and August 1966, Igbos and other peoples who were attacked as 'Easterners', it was **Lt. Col. Chukwue-**

meka Odumegwu Ojukwu. He had definitely heard about the horrific ways in which officers and men from that region were killed. Some, locked up in a guardroom, possibly for their own protection, had grenades tossed into the room and blown to bits by those determined to kill them. The mass killings of soldiers soon spread to the streets in several cities as thousands of civilians were killed.

No group deserves to go through all of this, largely due to the actions, and inaction of Major General Ironsi as Head of State, and for taking over power in the first place.

The fact that there was no talk or possibility of bringing the very identifiable perpetrators of the horrendous crimes of Aure Paiko to justice was more than enough ground for any region to seek to leave the fraudulently created Nigerian State.

The Ndigbo embraced the emerging Nigerian State and the opportunities it provided and dominated the mid-cadre of the Officer Corps at the time of the Independence. Colonialism also opened up the previously insular, but very republican Igbo country, and the people, used to competition for ranking privileges within age groups and societies, poured out to take advantage of new frontiers.

The first military coup happened within a year of Ironsi at the helm of the Nigerian Military. Ironsi, who had been ranked 3rd (among 3 candidates) for the job by the departing GOC was appointed to the position based on the insistence of Governor-General Azikiwe, as he and Prime Minister Balewa tried to resolve the several issues they were bickering over.

As such, the outcome of the first coup, opened the door for a boatload of questions, especially as two of Nigeria's (four) indigenous generals (and another full Colonel) were dead, with a third in London as the Defense Attache. There was thus no ranking military voice to oppose Ironsi's takeover or propose options for the Nigerian State at this time. Ifeajuna's insistence that Ademoyega not handle the critical task of eliminating Ironsi, only gave credence to the suspicion that Ironsi was the hand behind Ifeajuna.

The delay or failure to try the coupists led to growing dissension within the Military, and the Unitary tendencies of the Ironsi regime (including the interference in the Northern region civil service requirements, which Lt. Col Ojukwu suggested would provide more opportunities) increased the anxiety of Northern opinion leaders.

This was why many NCOs and officers from the middle-belt areas, with homelands experiencing of the expansionist tendencies of the Fuduyan Fulbe rulers of Hausaland (Tivs for instance), participated in 'Aure Paiko', but were not keen to be part of Murtala's conclusion to Operation Araba,

This in no way attempts to blame the victims of 'Auta Paiko,' but it is useful to provide the proper context to these tragic events.

Considering that there was no central purpose or underlying reason for the creation of Nigeria other than the plundering of the indigenous countries by foreigners, the demand for Biafra was certainly reasonable.

Too much consequence is often placed on Aburi. Gowon was in a position of strength as far as Nigeria and Biafra was concerned, but was in a position of great weakness as far as Nigeria and Arewa (operation Araba was concerned). You always have to consider your opponent's strategic choices, but Ojukwu seemed to show little sensitivity to the fact that

Gowon had to deal with Murtala, the Bello-Ribadu Officers, and the bulk of the Army NCOs.

The Aburi Accord (Decree 8) seemed to focus too much on what was meant to be an interim Military arrangement (Military Administrators and the Head of State), but the meeting was a start.

Ojukwu's failure to attend the ratification in Benin City where they could have ironed out differences (subsections 70 and 71, which gave Gowon controlling rights of the situation), and agreed on something, anything, that would have been much better than a bloody 30 month killing and destruction spree.

Coming to Benin with Banjo in tow, would have been an opportunity for Ojukwu to link up with Gowon, and Ejoor, now Military of the Mid-West, created by plebiscite as Nigeria's fourth region in 1963. Surely, Ojukwu and the three he tried to recruit to what would have been Nigeria's first coup a few years earlier, would have enough common ground for a side meeting to iron out personal issues and find a way to prevent the catastrophic war.

Yakubu Gowon and Emeka Ojukwu in Aburi, Ghana

The situation before these young men was not one of course mates seeking equal share. It was the lives and well-being of millions. Ojukwu believed himself to be superior to Gowon with a very good basis. He was the Oxford educated officer, who had joined the Army after a couple of years working as a civilian. His joining the Army as an NCO, was to rebel against what he felt was his millionaire father's influence over his life.

As such, in terms of experience, and the rank and commission he felt he would have had, if he made the decision to join the Military earlier, he was Gowon's senior.

It didn't help that Gowon, who Ojukwu viewed as inferior, had now been negotiated into position as Head of the Nigerian State. This was not a Military Commission; it was a quick arrangement by the creators and owners of Nigeria.

Murtala Muhammad as the swordsman of the Fuduyan Fulbes (also known as 'Northern Nigeria,' but with the recently created the term 'Hausa-Fulani' now adopted), Francis Cumming-Bruce, representing the English Colonials, who brought Albert Mathews with him.

Mathews was Ambassador of the United States, the global superpower to which the English were now subservient, but who generally viewed African matters in deference to England and France or from an Anti-Communist or Anti-Socialist perspective.

The Civil servants were also there to take care of the paperwork, after the fact.

As such, despite the extremely tragic and upsetting circumstances, Ojukwu needed to view the situation, and Gowon, for what it was, and not keep making counter broadcasts and demands that would probably not be met. He had accepted an extra-Military arrangement as Governor under Ironsi. He could not publicly turn around and start insisting on Military ranking and seniority in this extraordinary situation, except he was demanding the end of the Nigerian State, and prepared to follow through with it, and take on everyone (and Nation) that had negotiated the Gowon "solution."

A lot more could have been done privately though, and Benin was an opportunity for that. David Ejoor, who was certainly not subservient to Gowon was hosting.

Ejoor and Banjo in training as Cadets. Banjo led the Biafran Army in its most significant advancement into Benin, where Ejoor was military Governor. Banjo's concern about the capacity and discipline of his troops to execute an advance on Lagos, reportedly led him to attempt an authorized negotiated solution to the war, again from Benin. He was executed shortly afterwards.

Gowon the Statesman would have been partly driven by self-preservation instinct, like just about everyone. He was inexperienced and limited in political matters, but he was sincere, brave and conciliatory. The caliber of people and forces settling on him as leader of the Nigerian State also meant that Murtala had been told to stand down, and let Gowon operate.

It was now time to reach out to his old friend and course mate, and try to work things out.

Positions and interests were changing very quickly in these times. The middle-belt officers for instance, despite clear anger and opposition to Ahmadu Bello's incursions to Tivland, had participated in 'Aure Paiko'. One of them, Lt. Pam, eager to avenge his brother's death, triggered the whole thing off. They however had no interest in the 'Operation Araba' conclusion of the process. That was for the Fuduyan Fulbe's, their Hausa subjects, and maybe the Kanuris.

Gowon and Ojukwu: The young men who needed to find a way to prevent carnage.

Gowon just needed time, and perhaps privacy, with his old friend, who, by the way had invited him and Banjo to be part of a plot supposedly linked to the President, a couple of years back. It was in this spirit that Gowon went to Aburi. Ojukwu was however prepared. Gowon had clearly deviated from the objective of those who put him in office, with the Aburi (Accord) agreement, so a slightly different variant was released.

Ojukwu and Gowon: Those young men are gone, and all that was left, were these old men.

Ojukwu's press conferences, counter conferences and insults on Gowon continued. Some have jokingly suggested that Gowon's enrolment in a doctorate following his removal as Head of the Nigerian State, flowed from deep pain over Ojukwu's insults.

It seemed Ojukwu did not realize who had the advantage, in terms of military might and foreign support. Benin City, not Aburi was the last opportunity to avoid even more tragedy and carnage, and one man, who was completely outside the process officially, had the credibility and influence to set these young men, who were now bickering over everything, including who should take the credit for releasing him from prison, on the right path.

Obafemi Awolowo had been through a very rough 12 to 15 years. He had been seemingly harassed, double crossed, betrayed, stabbed in the back and eventually jailed by anyone and everyone that seemed to matter in the Nigerian State, and its colonial predecessor.

He spent most of the 50s trying to resist the alliance that was being instigated by the English Colonials with the Fulbe rulers of Hausaland represented by Ahmadu Bello's NPC, preferring to build his own political base by collapsing areas and divisions like Offa, Kabba and Ilorin into their natural home country, and building alliances with Joseph Tarka and the UMBC.

However, by similar logic of ethnic nationalities, facts of history and geography, the Western region and Awolowo were also vulnerable to threats of natural partition and division within its region. Many divisions on the eastern front of the region, including the areas of Asaba, Ibusa, Ogwashi-Uku formed the Anioma and Ika areas of Igbo (speaking) country[32]. It should be pointed out that several notable advocates of the 'Igbo-speaking' school of thought, including Philip Asiodu, now suggest that these groups, especially the Anioma, are Igbo, and not just Igbo speaking[33].

As such, it was not surprising that the peoples in these communities wanted out of the Western region, as did the Western Ijaw and Urhobo communities and ethnicities, with Dennis Osadebey (Anioma-Igbo) and Samuel Mariere (Urhobo), becoming the Premier of the Mid-Western region.

The reality of Colonialism, and the regions it created, and indeed the Nigerian State itself, was that previously unaffiliated communities were lumped into legal, fiscal and geographical entities.

The Action Group recognized the desire and agitation for a Mid-West region, and had moved a motion in 1955 for the creation of **Ben**in and **Del**ta[34]. It was hoping that it would make the move, shortly after independence, as the party in control of the country in a likely alliance with the NCNC.

Awolowo did not oppose the move, but was not in favor of the Benin province, Akoko-Edo and Warri being part of the Mid-West region.

The move to restore the Olu of Warri title, as it was reportedly previously known and likely influenced by the Ologbosere (traditional Prime Minister) Ogbemi Rewane, only seemed to infuriate the Ijaw and Urhobo communities in the town and area.

Awolowo had emphasized utmost respect and preservation of the cultural institutions, even as society quickly needed to modernize and develop. He however soon had to placate the Oba Akenzua of Benin (Omo n'Oba N'Edo) who was showing strong NCNC leanings and support for the Mid-West State with Benin City as the Capital.

Awolowo had already deposed the Alaafin and lost a key ally to a clash with a traditional ruler[35]. Taking on the Oba of Benin (who alongside the Alaafin & the Ooni could be regarded as the Cardinal Monarchs of a region with about 30 other ranking Monarchs) would be unwise, and on a personal level, the Midwest region would literally separate him from two of his closest allies, Anthony Enahoro and Aurthur Prest.

Anthony Enahoro, Alfred Reware (younger brother of the Ologbosere of Warri), Obafemi Awolowo and Arthur Prest

Eventually several aligned interests (Akintola battling for survival, NPC and NCNC support and strong support of the citizenry, with over 95% of the votes supporting the plebiscite and new region) led to the creation of the Midwest region, and shortly afterwards, Awolowo and Enahoro ended up in jail, along with most of the rest of the AG leadership.

The Action Group had been universally acknowledged for proving that excellence in African Governance, that quickly translates to an improvement in the lives of its people, while preserving or even enhancing the role of indigenous cultural and traditional institutions (admittedly, having much deeper significance in its region than elsewhere in the Nigerian State) was possible.

Despite general ambivalence towards the Nigerian State, it believed it had a path to the leadership of that State. This included a consolidation of its core base, reeling in the parts of its base that were gerrymandered into other regions, and getting a coalition on its own terms (not on Foreign English Colonial or Fuduyan Fulbe terms) with the NCNC.

With Dr. Azikiwe's volte-face and preference to be junior partner to the NPC, and internal dissention from Akintola and Fani-Kayode, the party, and its leaders were easy pickings for several opposing parties with an interest that only seemed to converge in enmity for the Action Group.

But here was Awolowo in late 1966, out of prison, and with enough credibility to bring the bickering young men together. Could he succeed where even the likes of Haile Selassie and other African leaders had failed with Ojukwu and Gowon?

While it is unlikely that Awolowo would have wanted to be involved with an English led (or influenced) intervention, it is also unlikely that Gowon would have invited Awolowo to his Government without notifying the English, at the very least.

Ojukwu's missing the Benin meeting, differences over what was agreed in the meeting between Ojukwu and Awolowo (an agreement not to secede, or not to announce secession yet) was claimed, and Gowon getting Mrs. Awolowo to put pressure on her husband eventually pushed Awolowo from an interventionist role to Finance Commissioner and unappointed strategist for the Nigerian side.

Benin City would have given Ojukwu, Gowon, Ejoor and Banjo to sort out whatever issues they had between and among them. Victor Banjo had again bizarrely offered or accepted to 'help out' in a government where he clearly was an outsider, and Ojukwu could have brought him to Benin for some recognized muscle on his own side of the negotiation table. Hassan-Katsina and Adeyinka Adebayo, were the other Military Governors at the Benin meeting.

Ojukwu's ignoring of the meeting of Gowon and the regional Governors in Benin, meant a hardening of stances, across board.

Gowon's decision to create 12 States by decree/military fiat, was the first of many by 'Northern' Military officers which has taken Nigeria to the current (as at 2021) 36 states, These states essentially function as branches of the Central Government, with the Constitution crafted by the military severely concentrating power in the Center through an over-reaching "exclusive" list.

Gowon's move in early May 1967 was clearly in bad faith, and an attempt to whittle Ojukwu's sphere of influence and create alternative administrative structures. Ojukwu responded towards the end of the month with the declaration of Biafra.

Regions of Nigeria
1963 - 1967

Awolowo did not go into the Gowon government alone. His allies from the first republic, Joseph Tarka, and Anthony Enahoro (also released from jail) held cabinet positions as well. The thought that Awolowo could have recommended either one of these fine gentlemen and stayed outside the fray lingers.

Enahoro, with Awolowo in the service of Gowon's Government

With a knack for efficient execution in governance, Awolowo quickly put the Nigerian State in what may be the strongest fiscal position it has ever been throughout its existence. A decade earlier, he needed to raise taxes to finance Universal Primary Education and Child Healthcare.

This time, Oil and a bit of strategy made it so much easier.

The four factors can be highlighted on how Nigeria's wartime government somehow managed to be in one of the best fiscal positions of its existence:

1. Get Revenues: Ojukwu wanted £2 million in monthly royalties from Shell BP. He had threatened sanctions but couldn't back it up as the companies offered an eighth of the amount demanded (£250,000). Awolowo was able to get the

companies to pay all the royalties to Gowon's government, which then enforced a sea blockade, and eventually quickly captured the oil producing Niger-Delta.

2. Efficiently allocate expenses to areas of need. Divisional Commanders were responsible for arms procurement for instance. This ensured there were no complaints about HQ procurements, and certainly limited the types and volume of leakages. There were probably still leakages, and Akinrinade suggested the divisional commanders were unnecessarily dragging the war on for financial reasons, which made the mid-rank officers reach out to officer-brothers across the line to end hostilities. Compare this to the situation (in 2017) where undelivered arms contracts worth a quarter of a billion dollars are awarded to the right type of 'migrant or stagnant' foreigner. A Nigerien this time.[36]

3. Accountability and Savings: The 'spend or squander it all' mentality of future Governments was absent. With Awolowo at the helm, the Government reportedly saved £990,000 that was due each month to the newly created East Central State (much higher than the Oil companies offered Ojukwu) and handed it over at the end of the War.

4. Delegation and Support: Awolowo also had the support of the 'Super Perm Secs, including Asiodu and Arikpo who fell in line behind the experienced Administrator. The Federal side was thus unexpectedly efficient, while Biafra seemingly tended towards dictatorship.

Despite Awolowo's achievements for the Nigerian State, there are genuine questions regarding the fact that he help create, or stabilize, the Central/Federal Government as the "monster" that is the primary revenue collection agency, and then distributes to the sub-national branches (States) it arbitrarily created as it deems fit.

His defenders will argue that the 12 states were created before he became part of Gowon's government, but Awolowo should have had the big picture, and needed to find a way to make it happen, despite the relative inexperience of Ojukwu and Gowon.

Murtala soon bungled his way out of relevance (going abroad for a short while) following a couple of spectacular war errors, flowing from his stubbornness and not realizing that conventional warfare was different from catching brother officers and soldiers by surprise in their homes and barracks.

The fiscal and revenue generating arrangements that were put in place by Awolowo, was for a Nation at war, and countering a seceding component. The process to reverse this ad-hoc arrangement, which remains largely in place as at 2024 till date (2021) should have been implemented, rather than perpetuate the monster that encourages laziness and corruption, and discourages productivity and sustainability for the countries trapped in the Nigerian State. Sustainability was hardly a factor for the States (branches of the Central Government) created by military.

Awolowo was also able to provide grants to the African Continental Bank, and the Cooperative Bank of Eastern Nigeria to help small business owners kick things off, after the war. The change in currency, like securing the oil revenues at the start of the war, proved critical in limiting the ability of the Biafran State. Ojukwu would probably have wanted an opportunity to undo, or unsay whatever it was that pushed the hardly temperamental, but straight shooting and straight talking Awolowo, over the line, from mediation to working with Gowon.

Awolowo's service to the Nigerian State, also came with personal image, and reputational blows, as his response to Biafran soldiers diverting food aid meant for the populace was to suggest a complete shutdown of the food aid program to squeeze the Biafran Army, since the food reportedly wasn't getting to the populace. No amount of explanation or pleas for forgiveness can excuse the suggestion and execution of starvation as a war policy, even if it is said to have helped end a war that should have been prevented at all costs.

The exchange of Biafran currency, whose exchange value, basis for printing and volume in circulation, could not be determined, was also problematic, but it is not uncommon for fiat money issued by a troubled state to become worthless.

Hopefully, this stark history will not be repeated for citizens of Nigeria, as the naira is something of a freefall in 2021, with the top treasury official adding petrol to the fire by removing transparency from what is the 'real market' for everyone not benefitting from the official 'arbitrage, round tripping' system. There must be an effort to introduce transparency and efficient allocation mechanisms for the exchange of the local currency for foreign currencies.

It could not be verified if the old Nigerian currencies were traded in, as there would be no excuse for that not to have been done. The fact that the change of currency severely affected the Biafran State also raises questions about the level of adoption of the Biafran Pound.

Awolowo stepped down from Gowon's government in 1971, and he was replaced by Fuduyan Fulbe key player,

Shehu Shagari, who had joined the cabinet in an economic development role, after the civil war in 1970. As expected, fiscal discipline and savings soon gave way to Cement Armadas[37], with unbelievable demurrage terms, and general wastage. Despite increased oil earnings, the nation began to experience financial trouble from around 1973, and had major problems financing the Delta steel company, Aladja in 1979[38]

Serving in the war cabinet with close pre-independence allies should have been an opportunity to jointly prepare and strategize for the political process, whenever it returned, if it ever did.

However, in 1979, neither Enahoro nor Tarka, even bothered joining forces with Awolowo's UPN, preferring to go with Shagari's NPN. Aper Aku emerged as Governor of Tarka's home State of Benue, on the banner of NPN, while Ambrose Alli became Governor of Enahoro's Bendel State on the banner of UPN, presumably without Enahoro's support.

The Nigeria of 1979 had been further splintered into 19 States a few years earlier by Murtala Mohammed, as military dictator.

The only position for Enahoro in Awolowo's UPN would have been that of the Presidential candidate, with Awolowo taking a role on the sidelines in a party building and/or advisory capacity.

Instead, the 70-year-old Awolowo, and the 75-year-old Azikiwe, were trying to create an alliance, two decades behind schedule.

While younger comrades and jailed 'Action Group' members like Lateef Jakande and Victor Onabanjo became Governors of Lagos and Ogun State, Awolowo's run for President in 1979 raised questions about his legacy.

Azikiwe, with Awolowo, met regarding the 1979 elections.

There were no questions about his motives. He wanted to do good and knew how to deliver. Most times, there were no questions about his methods as well. They were practical, straightforward, and efficient. There were however genuine questions on why he had to be the party leader and Presidential candidate at 70, during the 1979 elections.

He had been praised for focusing on his region in the 1950's and generally avoiding the mess that Nigeria was obviously going to become. The English Colonials were shocked by his choice to go to the Center, as opposition leader in the first republic, to 'facilitate a healthy democracy,' according to him. Maybe he always had Nigeria on his sights, and the move to the center was to await the collapse of the very poorly performing, and struggling coalition, so as to be right there to pick up the pieces when the political collapse eventually happened.

Ifeajuna and company happened instead.

Post Civil War History (1970-2024)

1970 - Gowon made a 'No Victor, No Vanquished' declaration regarding the war, and launched a 'Rehabilitation, Reconstruction and Reconciliation' program for the country. A four-year development plan was also launched.

General Yakubu Gowon

1971 - Awolowo resigns as Finance Minister and unofficial Vice President. Gowon said he (Awolowo) had helped Nigeria get out of financial disaster, and finance the war from internal resources, without debt, or devaluation of the currency.

Enahoro and Tarka also served in Gowon's wartime Cabinet. Awolowo is replaced as Finance Minister by Shehu Shagari.

1974 - Gowon postpones the planned handover date to civilian rule from 1976 to an unstated time in the future. Student protests on university campuses led to the closure of universities.

1975 - The Bello-Ribadu Officers led by Yar'Adua decided that it was time to take over 'their' country and approached Gowon's Brigade of Guards commander, Colonel Joseph Garba with their plans and an Ironsi type ultimatum; He (Garba) could make it easy and bloodless, or difficult, which mean bloody. Either way, they were going to succeed, and he had a choice either to work with them or to try to stand against them, and be consumed by events. The '75 coup, though eventually bloodless, has been described as the most intriguing in Nigeria's history, with a lot of twists and turns, including the eventual timing of the coup to when General Gowon was attending the OAU conference.

Just like in July 66 when he had to shuttle between the Ikeja Cantonment base of the coupists led by Murtala, and the Government's resistance led by Gowon, Garba was once again right in the middle between Gowon, the man he had sworn to protect, and Murtala, the man the coupist were trying to install.

There was a strange turn when General Gowon's plane suddenly returned from Uganda, but it was Gowon's aide-de-camp (ADC), Lt. Col. William Walbe, returning to get some documents for Gowon. Garba tracked Walbe to his home & with a truckload of soldiers outside, spoke to Walbe about their long association from their days as 'Boy Soldiers' in the Nigerian Military School, with a plea not to get killed by fighting the Coup[39].

Colonel Joe Garba, Col William Walbe

The coup eventually succeeded and General Murtala Muhammed, who was conveniently out of the country as the final phase of the coup played out, was allowed to fly back home (despite a closed Airport) to take the reins of power[40].

A final twist played out after the success of the coup as the plotters turned on their mentor, Murtala Muhammed, and demanded a power sharing arrangement, which in Nigeria usually means some form of direct access to the treasury. Murtala, who held the 'juicy' Communications portfolio under Gowon, was so upset about the demands for power-sharing and offices to be held[41] that he was willing to give up the offer to become the head of state. The intensity of that negotiation meeting seemed to have had a deep impact on Murtala Muhammed, as questions over identity and origins seemed to stir him to see himself as a Nigerian, rather than a swordsman of the foreign hegemony that has always sought control of the Nigerian State.

The reality of those negotiations however led to a complete clearance of the top echelons of the civil service, and expectedly, the military. This 'treasury accessing' clearance has been blamed [42] for the normalization of corruption and the disruption of the development[43] of the country. However, this type of diagnosis, though correct at some superficial level, only addresses the symptoms and not the root causes of the deep issues facing the Nigerian State, as we have seen.

Murtala tried to play a unifying role during his short time as head of state, forging an impressive non-aligned, pan-African identity and outlook for Nigeria, a radical change from the divisive and sectional stance he had taken in public life before that moment. He was particularly close to Colonel Ibrahim Taiwo (known as Ibrahim Kagara earlier in his military career) as both were devoted swordsmen of the hegemony who faced identity questions. Both were also accused of involvement in the Asaba massacre. Sadly, the fate of both men was tied in another tragic twist as they were felled by assassin's bullets on February 13, 1976, during a coup led (or announced) by Lt. Col. Buka Suka Dimka.

Gen. Murtala Muhammed and Col. Ibrahim Taiwo

1976 - In February of 1976, General Murtala Muhammed, Colonel Ibrahim Taiwo, and a few other officers lost their lives[44] in an attempted coup that was primarily carried out by middle-belt officers of Benue-Plateau origin against the regime of Murtala Muhammed. The coup eventually failed and the coup announcer, Colonel Buka Sukar Dimka was arrested in Abakaliki[45] and tried in Lagos. About 30 other officers and men of the military and the police and a few civilians were executed for their roles in the coup[46]. General Illiya Bisalla, the Commissioner of Defense at the time, was also mentioned and implicated by Colonel Dimka in the coup, although his involvement, and that of some of the other executed officers, including Joseph Gomwalk have been questioned.

In most other circumstances, General T. Y. Danjuma would have assumed the role of head of state (Yar'Adua could have also made an aggressive and audacious move). However, as the coup was mostly carried out by middle-belt officers (to reinstall Gowon according to some, including the Government, even if this was unlikely), it was difficult to make T. Y. Danjuma, also from the middle-belt, the executors and intended beneficiary of the coup that took out a strong representative of the Fuduyan Fulbe hegemony.

As such, the lot fell on General Olusegun Obasanjo, who was extremely reluctant and some say, fearful to take the position. Obasanjo bent backwards to try to placate the Hegemony, and one of his very first decisions taken was to award a double promotion to Shehu Musa Yar'Adua from Lt. Col to Brigadier General[47]. This was to make Yar'Adua the Chief of Staff Supreme Headquarters, thus bypassing dozens, if not scores, of his superiors in the army. Obasanjo continued to placate the Hegemony, primarily through the Bello-Ribadu officers, for instance, Muhammed Buhari, was made the petroleum minister (Federal Commissioner at the time).

Yar'Adua and Buhari had leading roles in the Murtala Coup and the Obasanjo Government

Shehu Musa Yar'Adua, with an aristocratic background as the son of the former Lagos Affairs minister in the first republic was undeniably ambitious, and it was obvious that Obasanjo greatly deferred to him and the other Bello-Ribadu Officers. As these things play out, there is never enough space at the top, and other Bello-Ribadu boys were on the outside, looking in (possibly with scorn). Sani Abacha and Tunde Idiagbon for instance, reportedly tried to instigate their GOC in Ibadan, James Oluleye, to publicly dissociate the brigade from the coup, once Yar'Adua's leading role became obvious.

Shehu Yar'Adua clearly attracted a lot of envy from his colleagues, contemporaries and officers from the far north, and this was to catch up with him much later on.

For instance, Ibrahim Babangida, as military head of state inexplicably excluded and removed Yar'Adua from the political process of the late 80s and early 90s.[48], while Sani Abacha imprisoned him. To the rest of the country, most of these gentlemen were beneficiaries of the Ribadu-Bello illegality, thus there was little reason for them to get upset or worked up by Yar'Adua enjoying extra privileges (like a double promotion) from the same type of illegality and nepotism, that they had all benefited from.

General Olusegun Obasanjo and Bri. Gen Shehu Yar'Adua

1979 - Obasanjo, in 1979, fulfilled his promise and handed over to a democratically elected civilian government. T. Y. Danjuma has said that as they (he, Yar'Adua, and Obasanjo) were leaving the army, he made sure that the army was left in the care of Alani Akinrinade, who became Chief of Army Staff[49]. Akinrinade has been credited by many, alongside other sub-commanders (including Alabi-Isama and Tomoye) as playing crucial roles in ending the civil war by proactively reaching out to officers on the Biafran side when it was became obvious that the fighting dragging on beyond what was necessary.

The military left governance in 1979 and General Akinrinade was named Chief of Army Staff, to help safeguard the civilian government. Danjuma also wanted Akinrinade to be Chief of Army Staff because he knew that the latter could handle the indiscipline and aggressive tendencies of the Bello-Ribadu Officers.

Obasanjo and Danjuma were glad to leave Office in 1979. This however made Yar'Adua's path to his ultimate objective a bit more complicated.

1980 - Fulbe Civilian President Shehu Shagari soon shot himself in the foot as he relieved Akinrinade of the command of the Army and 'demoted' him upwards, by creating a new role called the Chief of Defense Staff. Akinrinade resigned from the Army shortly afterwards and was replaced by Gibson Jalo, whose humiliation was probably worse than Akinrinade's, as Shagari created the role of Deputy Chief of Army Staff for Inuwa Wushishi. Jalo was relieved of his role after just over a year, and as such the men left behind (Southerner and wrong type of 'Northerner' in the books of the ruling clans) to contain the aggressive and unruly tendencies of the Bello-Ribadu crew had been pushed out by the man they were meant to protect.

Shagari, either listening to bad advice or taking bad decisions on his own, abolished the position of the Deputy Chief of Army Staff as soon as he got the 'right man' as Army Chief. He would soon get torched by the men his NPC bosses had forced into the Army in the 60's.

Shagari, Akinrinade, Jalo

1983 - Perhaps testing his limits of his 'command' structure, Buhari, then a Major General and GOC of the 3rd Armored Division in Jos defied the presidential order and invaded Chad, following incursions by Chadian troops into disputed border areas and islands around Lake Chad. The invasion almost reached the Chadian Capital N'Djamena. Shagari chose not to punish or reprimand his fellow Fulbe for the defiance.[50] An underlying reason for this may have been due to the fact that Hisen Habre's Toubou ethnic group have had a history of clashes with the Fulbe [51] across countries bordering the Sahara (Mali, Niger, Chad), and these key Nigerian State actors, were using Nigerian soldiers, weapons and resources to settle historical and foreign scores that mean absolutely nothing to indigenous Nigerians.

L: Brig General Ibrahim Bako with Major General Muhammadu Buhari, Head of State

1983 - On December 31, 1983, Brigadier-General Sani Abacha announced that there had been a coup removing the civilian government from office. Abacha, a Kanuri raised in Kano, finally emerged from the shadows. Abacha's background made him close to Muhammadu Buhari, leader of the coup, and a key swordsman of the hegemony over the years, but without the aristocratic background of Yar'Adua. Buhari, though Fulbe, had a Kanuri mother, and like Murtala and Taiwo before him, seemed eager to prove his devotion to the cause.

Buhari's coup has been said to be bloodless and was largely so. However, there were some intriguing deaths during the coup, especially that of Brig. Gen. Bako, who was rumored to have had a close relationship with the new head of state and was rumored to be the preferred choice as Chief of Army Staff. Buhari also enjoyed a much-laundered public image, thanks to the media influence of his older nephew, Mamman Daura.

1984 - 1985 - Despite its tough stance on indiscipline in public life, the Buhari administration proved to be clueless in changing the fortunes of the country and quickly plunged the country into serious economic crises. There were soon shortages of essential commodities, which then came under various forms of control.

1984 – In another tough public stance against corruption, Buhari ordered a change in the colors of all the Naira (fiat paper) currency ranging from ₦1 – ₦20 (between 1 naira and 20 naira) with a limited time for the public to change their currencies in banks. Among the reasons given was pull the rug from under the feet of people that had stashed money abroad. Guardian Nigeria journalist Okunaba Adinoyi Ojo reported that key Fulbe Clan leader from Gwandu, and father of Buhari's ADC, Major Mustapha Jokolo imported 53 suitcases, and soldiers had prevented the customs from carrying out the Presidential directive of searching all imported luggage. (The Gwandu based clan leader is ranked 2,3 or 4 by Hausaland's Fulbe rulers, depending on who is doing the ranking with Sokoto, Kano & Kanuri Shehu of Borno, who has not identified with the Fuduyan Fulbes, pulled into the rankings). Future Vice President and Presidential Candidate, Atiku Abubakar, was the Customs Station Manager for the Airport at the time.[52]

Buhari would instantly have his pound of flesh on the Guardian, as two of its journalists were jailed for "false statements likely to bring the government or officials into ridicule or disrepute."

Mrs. Ransome Kuti and Prime Minister Tafawa Balewa

1984 - In a clear contrast to the Gwandu suitcase affair, Fela Kuti is arrested with foreign currency while heading out of the country for a concert in the United States and tried in what the Guardian described as 'sham currency smuggling charges' and jailed for 5 years.[53] The judge later apologized and said he had been ordered to jail Kuti[54]. Fela's fearless and witty renditions on the Nigerian State had been a source of irritation for successive Military dictators. A few years earlier, his sprawling compound 'Kalakuta Republic' was invaded by soldiers and destroyed. Everyone present including his mother, famous activist Funmilayo Ransome-Kuti, was beaten and she later succumbed to her injuries. The order to invade the compound and get Fela 'dead or alive' was said to be right from the highest echelons of Nigeria's military dictatorship[55]. The Government commission of inquiry declared that it was the action of unknown soldiers.

L: Fela Kuti R: Customs Officer (later Vice President) Atiku Abubakar

1985 - Buhari's reaction to his inability to tackle growing economic hardship was to push the narrative of a disciplined and uncompromising enforcer, with obvious examples being the jailing of Guardian journalists (Nduka Irabor and Tunde Thompson) and the retroactive implementation of laws to execute drug traffickers. Buhari has often failed to comprehend the illegality of the executions with responses suggesting that questioning the execution was akin to supporting drug trafficking, but clearly failing to see the danger posed by a Government convicting any one based on a law that did not exist (or did not carry the implemented punishment) at the time of the act/misdemeanor or crime.[56]

1985 - Given the human rights records and economic struggles of the regime, including shortages of essential commodities, the removal of the Buhari junta in August 1985 was generally welcomed. Babangida's (AKA IBB) bloodless coup was filled with intrigue and against the odds in many regards. A non-Fulbe, his ethnic origin has been the subject of much debate and rumors with Kano, Bida, Minna and Ogbomosho offered as answers to questions about his ancestral home. This was important for officers joining the Army in the early 60's, given the 'ethnic camouflaging' of a few of the young men to pose as mostly Hausa (much tougher to disguise as Fulbe or Kanuri, the other ethnic beneficiaries) to take advantage of the Bello-Ribadu policy.

It was significant that Buhari's Service Chiefs (Bali, Aikhomu, Alfa, with IBB moving up from being Army Chief and replaced by Abacha) were retained by IBB, suggesting that they all sanctioned the removal of their Principal, or worse, a complete disenchantment and lack of trust in his ability to lead.

1985 - IBB's rise to power was probably due to his personal charisma and ability to rally and relate with subordinates in the military. His role in quelling the Dimka coup in 1976 also gave him leverage with the Bello-Ribadu stronghold within the Military, which was strongly linked to the Fuduyan Fulbe clans.

At the core of IBB's rise to power were a number of Lt. Col's and Cols. at the time (known as IBB Boys) including David Mark, Lawrence Onoja, Tunde Ogbeha, John Shagaya, Anthony Ukpo and Lawan Gwadabe. Most of these Officers were from the 'Middle Belt' but IBB's reach extended beyond the zone, and the role of Major Sambo Dasuki, a key member of Hausaland's ruling Fulbes in the coup is well documented. Dasuki served as IBB's ADC till he quit the position following a clash with Maryam Babangida and was sent out of the country on a course to douse the tension. Dasuki also later served as Goodluck Jonathan's National Security Adviser.

Many of the IBB boys smoothly transitioned to civilian life after being removed from the Army by (civilian President) Obasanjo with David Mark, John Shagaya and Tunde Ogbeha serving in the Nigerian Senate.

Part of the public's charm with IBB was also due to his wife. Nigerian leaders had mostly been distant and unengaging, and their wives were hardly in the public (outside of Victoria Gowon, who married the previously single General Gowon), but suddenly, there was Maryam Babangida who did not stay in the shadows but was very much beside her husband in the public. Her 'Better Life for Rural Women' program (with no clear budgetary funding source) provided an independent platform for public engagement, apart from just being the wife of the Military ruler. Her Asaba origins were also a factor in the thought that IBB could be a leader for all people, given the tragedy suffered by the town during the civil war.

Mrs. Babangida and a foreign dignitary, Princess Diana

However, as has been seen throughout the perilous History of the Nigerian Military and State, rallying younger officers and making promises to them while seizing power has little to do with the good or effective administering of the country. Nigerians were eagerly looking for some sort of competent leader to relieve the seemingly endless rot and grind of the country over the past decades, but IBB's charm and ability to draw everyone close and make promises to just about everyone quickly turned into weakness and disaster.

The term 'North' in Nigeria is often synonymous with the interests of Hausaland's foreign Fulbe rulers, and the clan leaders soon set to remind IBB that he was a beneficiary of the 'Northern' magnanimity through the Bello-Ribadu policy. IBB quickly calmed this key power base by rejigging his cabinet [57] and ruling council and having Nigeria take up a full membership of the OIC in 1986.

1986 - Mamman Vatsa, friend and course mate of Ibrahim Babangida (the latter was his best man at his wedding), notable poet, and the Minister of the Federal Capital Territory at the time was arrested with several other officers and executed for reportedly planning a coup. It was unique that some Air Force officers were implicated in the plot and executed. Many felt this was the path that started a long period of neglect of the Air Force [58]. And for over a decade, the graduating Air Force classes of the Nigerian Defense Academy did not go to flight school. This caused a generation gap of about a decade of pilots, which did not end until the restoration of democracy and the Olusegun Obasanjo Presidency, when the regular training of pilots restarted.

Dele Giwa, leading journalist and one of four founders of Nigeria's leading news magazine, NewsWatch, was killed via a letter bomb in his Lagos residence. IBB ridiculously stated afterwards that he did not investigate the killing due to a court order barring him from doing so [59].

1987 - Ibrahim Babangida created two states, Akwa Ibom and Katsina, shortly after taking office. He also created some more states in 1991 making him the only head of state to have created states twice within his administration. All states that have been created in Nigeria have been created by northern military generals, except the plebiscite that led to the creation of the Midwest state, which was aided by the deal between Akintola and the NCNC members of the Western House of Assembly during the Action Group crisis (1962-1963)[60].

1990 - A coup, announced by Tiv Major, Gideon Orkar attempted not just to overthrow the government, but also to excise the far north (Hausa and Kanuri countries), from the rest of Nigeria. It was the third time since 1966 that military officers had tried to carve out territory and forcefully partition the country. The first was the attempt by Col. Murtala Mohammed to remove the 'North,' as he determined it, from Nigeria, and the second, was the Biafra war when Colonel Ojukwu tried to remove the southeast from the country. The Orkar coup was crushed, reportedly with the Chief of Army Staff Sani Abacha playing the lead role in quelling it[61]. The varied reactions to the Orkar Coup perhaps highlighted the sharp differences and divisions that exist in the country.

Perhaps the reaction or the writings of respected journalist, Kabiru Gwangwazo showed the schism that exists in the country on this matter. In a series of articles he has written on the coup, titled "Gideon Orkar's Madness," he mentioned that working at a media house at the time, all the journalists from the other parts of the country rejoiced at the thought that the coup was successful.

The feeling on the streets at the thought of the excision of the far north from the country certainly matched that in the Triumph newsroom with the general sentiment that the 'troublers' of the rest of the country had been excised. In Gwangwazo's own words, *"For me, then a reporter/sub-editor, at The Triumph newsroom, a mini-Nigeria of a news hub, the unenlightened response to the Orkar lunacy by almost all of my non-Muslim colleagues, especially from the Middle-Belt and the Igbo East, in particular, was a painful eye-opener. I understand, for IBB too, it was an eye-opener."*[62] Gwagwazo seemed particularly pained that 'Middle Belters' were leading and celebrating the attempt to split Nigeria, and this shows the very unenlightened (using his own words), but extremely worrying perspective of many of the 'Northern' elite and intellectuals who seem determined to close their eyes to the issues staring at them right in the face, which is that Hausa Country under foreign Fulbe control, and to some extent Kanuriland, when willing to enter into a partnership with the foreign Fulbes, has mostly been a source of trouble, burden and threats to the rest of the indigenous Nigerian countries have been forced into the Nigerian State with them.

Gwagwazo then continues and says the *'holistic and unified Northern Nigeria' finally and effectively came to an end. That was when that Northern unity was killed. IBB was obviously the main reason for that murder so gruesome. This is despite his being a principal beneficiary of the' 'Monolithic North bequeathed us by the North's Sardauna Ahmadu Bello, managed effectively and efficiently by our successive leaders.*

Without doubt, the Orkar coup attempt was madness and doomed to fail because the odds were stacked against it.

For starters, nobody has the right to murder or execute anyone while unilaterally playing judge, jury and executioner, whether it'd be Nzeogwu, Dimka, Orkar or Murtala and the bulk of the Bello-Ribadu crew who murdered over 200 of their colleagues in Ikeja, Abeokuta, Ibadan and other parts of Nigeria.

A coup done the 'right way' is a thankless, no reward, full risk endeavor as the plotters will have to arrest their targets without any bloodshed, and then hand them over to the police or command structure, while surrendering to the same authorities for insurrection. In effect, there is no right way to carry out a coup. That is why conversations about governance and societal arrangements must be thorough, frank and not suppressed.

Nigeria's current constitutional arrangement baselessly and hilariously comes to the conclusion that Nigeria is one indivisible nation (Section 2) with little consideration for its extremely shaky, if not outrightly fraudulent foundations. Sections 8 and 9 make it virtually impossible to achieve the much-needed constitutional change through the national assembly.

It must however be pointed out that no violent coup has succeeded (on its own) in Nigeria's troubled history, and once you throw violence and murder into the mix, the dynamics can quickly get out of control.

- In January 1966, Nwobosi arrested Fani-Kayode, but executed Akintola even after he surrendered, due to the initial resistance put up. Almost all the other plotters resorted to violence as the first resort. The takeover attempt was stalemated (unless you go with the narrative that Ironsi was pulling the strings on Ifeajuna all along and stepped in as planned), and the coupists had to surrender.

- The unpunished acts of July 1966 were not a takeover attempt, but acts of war against what would soon be a foreign country. These plans also ended in a stalemate, with senior civil servants, Yakubu Gowon and the English Ambassador stepping in to end the imbroglio, and 'negotiations' rooted in selfish interests producing Yakubu Gowon to try to save the Nigerian state for reasons that have nothing to do with the good and benefit of indigenous Nigerians.

- The Dimka coup of 1976 was unsuccessful, with IBB earning 'brownie points' with the power base for his role in quelling the coup.

Coups in Nigeria go beyond a group of young men shooting their way to the TV and Radio house and killing a couple of politicians along the way. Almost nobody will hear a speech on NTA these days anyway and so maybe the next set of plotters will upload a YouTube video or send WhatsApp messages!

That is why the bloodless coups (especially Yar'Adua's on Gowon) have had the most intrigue, and even with IBB's overthrow of Buhari (which was more of an indictment of Buhari by all his top Generals, apart from Idiagbon), Babangida was quickly reeled back in to do the bidding of the power base that believes it owns Nigeria. The support of the top military brass was not sufficient for effective control of the country.

While the plan for Orkar's coup was madness and not grounded in reality, the sentiment behind the coup was very much sane, logical and in some ways predictive, as the states excised by Orkar, somewhat mirrored the states that 'removed' themselves from the secular Nigerian Nation with the declaration of Sharia law just over a decade later. It is certainly much saner than the logic that assumes that a nation set up by, for (the benefit of) and controlled by foreigners with no cultural or historical links to the indigenous peoples and ethnicities, must exist as 'one indivisible nation' that takes the right and opportunity for self-determination away from the indigenous peoples.

Orkar's coup speech (like all others) had some laughable and ridiculous aspects, and the forced removal of legal residents from any part of the Nigerian state must never happen (invading foreign AK47 wielding terrorists occupying forests reserves do not meet the criteria of legal residents). However, a demand in the speech was quite telling.

"To send a delegation led by the real and recognized Sultan Alhaji Maccido to the federal government to vouch that the feudalistic and aristocratic quest for domination and operation will be a thing of the past and will never be practiced in any part of the Nigeria state."

Orkar was in essence requesting that the Fulbe rulers of Hausaland should be content with their 'prize' and stop using it as a launchpad to harass and bother the rest of the country. Seems sane and logical enough!

Getting back to Gwangazo, what is even crazier than Orkar's coup is to think that there has ever been a 'Monolithic North' and then have the confidence, not just to say it, but put it in print.

Lugard decided to add the 'middle belt' to the far North to achieve fiscal balance to a Hausa country that had been turned from one of Africa's richest to one of its poorest within 100 years of rule by the foreign Fulbe clans (this impoverishment or 'constraint to development' is common to many forms of colonialism). I wonder how he could suggest the North was monolithic,

- When Ahmadu Bello reasoned that it was better (for him) to be dead than be Hausa. How monolithic was that north?
- Or when he mentioned that the Tivs were his grand-father's slaves? The appointment of an administrator (Aliyu Muhammed) and the use of the Army to sub-jugate the Tivs and eliminate efforts at self-determina-tion were among the reasons stated by the January '66 coupists for their actions.
- Prime Minister Tafawa Balewa certainly didn't think the North was Monolithic. Not when his grandmother told him every night as a child that he had a responsi-bility to 'kill the Fulani and drive them from our land' when he grew up.
- Maybe he is referring to the North, where even in the Fulbe ruled Hausaland, the Maguzawa have been largely alienated within their own country and even

somewhat stripped of their ethnicity, one of the most basic forms of identity.

If we limit the definition of monolithic to large, slow to change (it has actually rapidly retrogressed and is dragging the other countries in the Nigerian state with it) and add 'subjugated by foreigners' to the mix, then Gwangazo and others who love to repeat this 'monolithic north' line, may be right.

However, despite Lugard's gift to Hausaland's Fulbe rulers aligning with his own need to social climb in England, and subsequent fraud and gerrymandering by the colonials for reasons previously stated, there has never been one Monolithic North. There is one Hausa Country though, and it is currently split across borders that were fraudulently and artificially created in Berlin. Little wonder why the proponents of the Monolithic North always seem to miss the elephant in the room while chasing phantoms.

1990 - Ibrahim Babangida moved the Federal Capital to Abuja, in the middle of Nigeria, mostly created from Gbagyi and Nupe countries. The process was started by Murtala Muhammed based on the results of the Akinola Aguda panel in 1975.

1990 - Ibrahim Babangida moved the transition to civil rule to 1993, from 1990 and launched two political parties, the progressive-leaning Social Democratic Party and the conservative-leaning National Republican Convention. He also banned a few people, including Gen. Shehu Musa Yar'Adua (Rtd.) from the political process[63].

1992 - IBB's regime also witnessed the sad event of the C-130 crash in Ejigbo shortly after takeoff from Lagos Airport. Over 150 Nigerian military officers and 8 other officers from four African Countries (Ghana, Tanzania, Zimbabwe, Uganda) were killed in the crash.

1993 - Businessman Moshood Abiola wins the June 12, 1993, elections conducted by Ibrahim Babangida, but during the announcement of the results, the process was suspended and the elections later annulled. In IBB's own words, he annulled the elections because:

' *They do not trust me. Without Sani, I will not be alive today; without the North, I would not have become an officer in the Nigerian Army and now the President of Nigeria I don't want to appear ungrateful to Sani; he may not be bright upstairs but he knows how to overthrow governments and overpower coup plotters. He saw to my coming to office in 1985 and to my protection in the many coups I faced in the past, especially the Orkar coup of 1990 where he saved me and my family including my infant daughter. Sani risked his life to get me into office in 1983 and 1985; if he says he does not want Chief Abiola, I will not force Chief Abiola on him'.* [64]

By 'the North,' IBB is of course referring to the foreign Fulbe rulers of Hausaland who adopt the 'Northern' title when it is time to exercise control over the Nigerian state, with religion sometimes used as the trump card. His stated indebtedness regarding the Army dates back to the Bello-Ribadu policy of the early 60's, the reason Nigeria's 'deep state' was able to reel him (IBB) in from about 1986.

For Abiola, it was the 2nd time his Presidential ambition had been truncated. In the 1979 - 1983 era, as a major backer and financier of the ruling party, he seemed to be under the impression that he would be the (NPN) Party's Presidential candidates at some point in the 80's, but since parties (and candidates) in Nigeria do not need outside private funding once elected, he was eased out of the party with those famous lines 'The Presidency is not for sale' by Shagari's Transport Minister, Umaru Dikko

Abiola may have assumed that the banning of other heavy-weights like Yar'Adua from the 1993 contest was a clearing of the path for him, but the rug was pulled from under his feet right at the finish line.

Abiola, an accountant, was the Nigerian head of ITT (a global Telecoms giant that was split up in the 90's and whose successor companies include The Hartford, Starwood Hotels and ITT Tech) who had struck up a close friendship with Communications Minister (Commissioner) and later Head of State, Murtala Mohammed. Murtala was Abiola's access not only to Communications, but also to key Military officers, especially the Bello-Ribadu power base. Abiola also started his own telecommunications company (RCN), even though he remained on the global board of ITT. He also delved into other business ventures, including Media with Concord Newspapers.

Abiola was criticized for his wheeler-dealer tendencies and personal excesses, with supporters responding that his personal life should be separated from public office and political ambition. While the personal affairs of public officers should be protected from the public space, there should be some accountability for personal conduct and demand for personal integrity and ethics. This is probably more necessary for Nigeria and its constituent countries or successor states, given the relatively weak systems and institutions. In addition to competence, those in charge of public affairs and the treasury must be men and women of integrity.

Anthony Enahoro (with Abiola) made a rare appearance (at the time) to condemn the 'annulment' of the 1993 electoral process.

As such, nobody seeking public office should have more than four biological children. Nobody seeking public office should have more than one spouse[65]. Public officials should be models and examples, given the challenge posed by a rapidly growing population. This limitation should apply to all public life including civil servants, legislators and contestants for and holders of political office. Situations where judges, legislators, civil servants and public executives have children by the dozens and wives and concubines that cannot be counted on a hand isn't just a recipe for corruption in governance, but an entrenchment of poverty for the general populace. Nigeria or its successor states, should they remain secular, must ensure that all public officials adhere to the single spouse, four children limit policy.

Abiola may also have sealed his fate when he vowed to demystify the National Oil Company, NNPC, which itself is an alternate, or off-balance sheet treasury for Nigeria's rulers and owners. He promised transparency in this key, but unnecessary and value destroying source of government revenue[66]. Almost 30 years later, NNPC's revenue is still as convoluted as it has always been as the organization continues to destroy value, with billions of dollars lost each year between the clear and straightforward revenue generated (petroleum profits from crude sales) and the remittance to the public treasury.

L: Abiola with Babangida R: Abiola with Abacha

1993 - Sani Abacha removes the Interim National Government from the scene via a bloodless coup. This ushers in a period of crazed and brutal dictatorship by another Bello-Ribadu beneficiary.

Abacha, the man who announced the initial Buhari coup had been a workhorse behind the scenes for various military coups. He probably felt that this was his time and his reward for serving various military juntas.

Former US military chief Colin Powell said Sani Abacha's CIA profile was the most troubling he had ever read[67]. But this should not be surprising, given the background of these officers who were forced into the Army by Ahmadu Bello and Ribadu in the 60's. The tendency is not to value what you did not earn, and these young men, who were likely not qualified to be officers in the army, ensured that Nigeria (at least the indigenous Nigerians, since the 'owners' tend to have an 'opposite people' (© Fela) mentality) paid a bitter price for Bello-Ribadu corruption of the Officer Corps of its Army.[68].

1993 - Sani Abacha appoints Allison Madueke as Chief of Naval Staff, the first Igbo service Chief since the end of the Nigeria-Biafra civil war. He was removed from office less than a year later.

Abacha and Babangida

1995 - Sani Abacha executes poet, playwright and writer, Ken Saro-Wiwa under circumstances that remain controversial to date. Abacha and Saro-Wiwa had known each other either during or shortly after the civil war and Abacha believed that he had assurances from his old friend Saro-Wiwa that there would be limited (or no more) activism in Ogoni land. Thus, he felt betrayed by Saro-Wiwa's continued activism.

Saro-Wiwa and 8 other activists were arrested and prosecuted on charges of the murder of other leaders in Ogoni land. Subsequent and independent investigation suggests that the murders were not ordered or committed by Saro-Wiwa, and it was a setup[69]. Many military officers, probably acting upon orders, played a very ignoble role in the Ogoni affair. Saro-Wiwa and his co-defendants were convicted by a special tribunal led by Justice Ibrahim Auta and notably, were executed even before the 30-day period that should have been allowed for an appeal of the conviction. The outcry, both local and foreign) over the executions was swift and massive.

L: Kenule Saro-Wiwa R: Nelson Mandela

1996 - Following criticisms from South African president Nelson Mandela[70], Gen. Sani Abacha crazily stopped the national team, the Super Eagles from attending the Nations Cup in South Africa. That generation of the Super Eagles was considered as one of the finest up to that point and were the defending champions of the tournament and would likely have repeated in South Africa, as shown by getting the Olympic gold in the same year in the Atlanta Olympics. Nigeria was subsequently banned from participating in the two following Nations Cup tournaments, prematurely ending the national team careers of some of the finest generation of Nigerian players that had been seen up to that point.

Abacha stopped the Super Eagles from defending their African title in South Africa in 1996 and were banned from the next Nations Cup. The Eagles were favored to win, and won Olympic Gold in the same year.

The Air Force continued to suffer from a shortage of young pilots and a reported lack of training for existing ones, supposedly due to an unwritten policy following the suspected participation of Air Force officers, who were to use fighter jets to execute the Vatsa coup. This may have come back to bite the country and its leaders in a very personal way, as pilot error was suspected in a number of military crashes, including one that claimed the life of Abacha's son, and other young Nigerians from notable families.

1997 - Shehu Musa Yar'Adua dies in Prison. Perhaps frustrated that opportunities for his shot at Nigeria's Presidency seemed perpetually delayed, Shehu Yar'Adua launched a public campaign against Abacha's plans to transition from military head of state to a civilian president. Sani Abacha locked Yar'Adua in jail and sadly, he was never going to get out again. Abacha had been adopted by all the political parties as the Presidential Candidate, and previously unknown personalities were suddenly driving well-funded and coordinated mass campaigns and rallies for Abacha. These included Yomi Tokoya and GESAM (General Sani Abacha Movement for Peaceful and Successful Transition) and Daniel Kanu and YEAA (Youth Earnestly Ask for Abacha). A couple of known and respected public personalities, including Daniel Amokachi, Danladi Bako, John Fashanu, Nwankwo Kanu and shockingly, Maitama Sule, also got involved in the Abacha for President effort.

1998 - Sani Abacha died unexpectedly a few hours after meeting PLO chairman, Yasser Arafat in Abuja. Abacha's CSO, Major Al-Mustapha suggested that Abacha was clandestinely poisoned by one of Arafat's security officers. Even though reports are murky and somewhat scandalous, Abacha is reported to have died later that night after hanging out with close pal, then FCT minister, General Jeremiah Useni[71].

Sani Abacha greets Yasser Arafat

The moments following Abacha's death sadly reflect how thin and shaky the foundations of the Nigerian State are, and why even the military's role as a basis for unity is flawed and distorted.

Abacha's Chief Security Officer (CSO), Al-Mustapha supposedly consults Ibrahim Babangida and other key 'Northern' figures and then calls a couple of senior officers (excluding Jeremiah Useni, who was the most senior officer, and had diligently fought for the foreign Fulbe hegemony (aka 'the North') since 'Aure Paiko', to the detriment of his own people in the Jos Plateau, according to some. The main figures consulted to decide who was going to become the next head of state were General Ibrahim Babangida and then Lagos administrator Buba Marwa (reportedly son of one last set of

'Glover's Hausas type soldiers (born in Lagos, but rabidly 'pro-hegemony' and anti-'South'). Abacha's wife supposedly favored Marwa, showing how a few people think they can (and do) decide the destiny of the Nigerian State because they have access to brute force and weapons to kill and intimidate indigenous peoples.

Al-Mustapha has subsequently stated 'they' had boys ready in Abuja and in surrounding places like Keffi to take over the country and could have, if he wanted, started a 'revolution' (He is obviously not a student of contemporary Nigerian History). He was reportedly talked out of doing so by Babangida.

Al-Mustapha also said that he considered shooting Abdusalami Abubakar, the man who was eventually selected by the group to become the head of state at a 9:00 am meeting the following morning, because Abubakar dared to sit on the chair of the late Sani Abacha.

The announcement of Abacha's death later that day set off scenes of instant and unplanned jubilation and street partying in the Middle Belt and the South of the Country, with Fulbe controlled Hausa, and Kanuri countries naturally taking the opposite stance.

Al-Mustapha, Jeremiah Useni and Abdulsalami Abubakar

1998 - About a month after Abacha's death, Moshood Abiola, who had been in detention for most of Abacha's regime was also reported dead in circumstances that have caused much speculation. Many felt it was an equalization and a settlement or an opportunity for a clean break from the past to give the nation a fresh start. Abiola reportedly took ill during a meeting with senior American diplomat and one time Ambassador to Nigeria, Thomas Pickering. A heart attack was stated as the official cause of death.

1998 - 1999 - The government of Abdusalami Abubakar proved to be truly transitional and set an aggressive timetable for itself to leave governance. Abdusalami is often blamed for bequeathing the 1999 constitution to the country, which a lot of people called a fraudulent and faulty constitution, but the truth is that Nigeria is a conglomerate of several countries and it cannot and should not have one constitution if it is to survive. Perhaps the biggest knock on Abdusalami's government was the 1999 constitution that he bequeathed to the country.

Gen. Abdusalami just did what he could do to manage a really bad situation and left the scene as quickly as possible. He wasn't expected to fix any of the deep flaws or foundational issues that the country has always faced.

1999 - At the end of Abdusalam's transition process, former military ruler Olusegun Obasanjo eased past Architect and Shagari's Vice President, Alex Ekwueme in the PDP primaries, and then defeated Yale educated Economist and former finance minister Olu Falae in the main elections. The answer to the electoral question was known to most before the test, and it was believed that Obasanjo's emergence was to compensate the 'South-West' of Nigeria, with a candidate from the region, but with a commitment to or consideration for the foreign hegemony, for the presidency that was denied to Moshood Abiola.

L: Ekwueme and R: Falae lost to Obasanjo at various stages of the 1999 elections

Obasanjo and Abiola hailed from the same town, Abeokuta (even if there are interesting Anambra suggestions regarding Obasanjo) where they were students at Abeokuta Grammar School at the same time. While he could not be described as a 'Fuduyan Swordsman' like the Bello-Ribadu group in the Army, he had certainly posed no opposition to the cause throughout his time as an officer in the Army, including as Head of State, and was definitely a much safer choice than his major contenders. According to Ekwueme:

"Obasanjo was in Yola Prison, he had no idea how we formed the party and what it was formed for, but they foisted him on us as a President and leader of the party"[2]

In Obasanjo, there was alignment between external powers and influencers, and Nigeria's internal foreign colonizers, who had gone too far, even by their own aggressive standards. It also appears that the Americans were directly interested in Obasanjo's candidacy, rather than the usual approach of leaving West African affairs to France and England. Obasanjo was in the good books of the Americans for his 1979 handover, and was close to Andrew Young, the former US ambassador to the UN, and maintained friendships with Jimmy Carter, the former US President and Walter Carrington, the former US ambassador to Nigeria.

With the amount of money available in Nigeria's shadow (Off-Balance Sheet) treasury, it was not difficult for those who foisted him on Ekwueme and Co. to fund his campaign and steamroll him to the Presidency.

Obasanjo takes over from Abdulsalam

Atiku Abubakar, Obasanjo's choice for Vice President was an interesting one. The post-Customs Atiku became the deputy leader of PDM (People's Democratic Movement) a platform (as opposed to a Party) that Yar'Adua had set up to actualize his long-standing Presidential ambition. Atiku had just won the election to become Governor of the curiously named 'Adamawa' state but gave that seat up to become Obasanjo's Vice President.

Atiku and Yar'Adua

Upon becoming president, one of Obasanjo's first moves was to retire all military officers who had held political positions; officers who had been ministers and military administrators or governors were retired from the military. This move was retroactively seen as probably saving the country, or at least keep it trudging along for another decade or so, until the fundamental issues return to the front burner. There was a lot of disaffection within the barracks at these(dollar) millionaire officers who combined wealth with ambition and military power. The decision to remove these political officers helped restore some camaraderie within the military and closed the chapter of the direct impact of the Bello-Ribadu stain on the Army.

1999 - Revelations during the Human Rights Commission (Oputa Panel), during accusations and counter-accusations by Abacha's military intelligence chief, Brig. Gen. Sabo and Chief of Army Staff, Ishaya Bamaiyi, and the chief security officer, Al-Mustapha revealed the depth of the brazen corruption, autocratic rule, and depravity of the Abacha regime. Abacha's government was notorious for crazy economic policies including issuing multiple official exchange rates. He was also notorious for parallel governance structures like the non-transparent and nepotistic petroleum trust fund, headed by Muhammadu Buhari, who has insisted Abacha was not corrupt[73], despite over \$4.6 billion [74] in stolen funds recovered. Expectedly, several key actors in clear corruption cases remain active in Nigerian public leadership as of 2021.

L: Gen. Sabo, C: Maikyau (SAN) R: Gen. Bamaiyi Maikyau's cross examination of Sabo was one of the highpoints of the Oputa Panel, revealing an underbelly of the top echelons of Nigerian leadership that most criminal organizations would be ashamed of

1999 - 2001 Extrajudicial killings are reported by the military under Obasanjo in Odi and Zaki-Biam[75].

2000 - 2001 A legal partitioning of the country sees 12 states implement Sharia law. The States roughly matched the those that were announced as excised during the Orkar coup attempt and roughly matched the sections of Hausa and Kanuri countries within Nigeria. The ensuing riots, especially in Kaduna, left thousands dead.

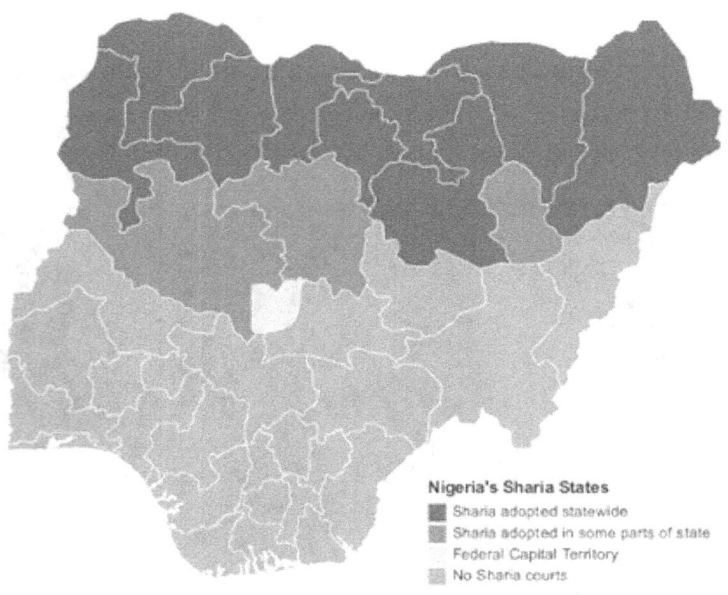

Nigeria's Sharia States

- Sharia adopted statewide
- Sharia adopted in some parts of state
- Federal Capital Territory
- No Sharia courts

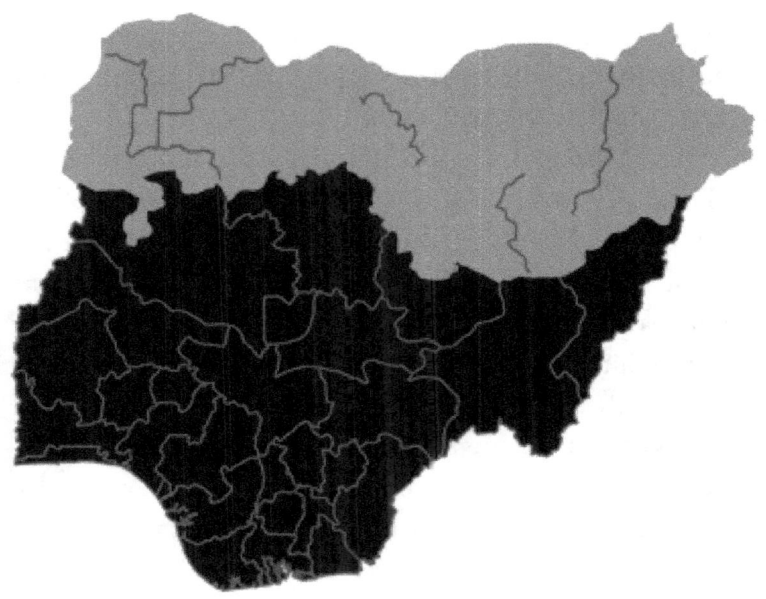

Orkar's announced partitioning/Excision in 1990

2001 - Obasanjo famously tried to sidestep the sharia issue and did nothing about it even though he was aggressive towards other constitutional violations such as the creation by Lagos State of LCDAs (Local Council Development Areas) alongside the Local Government Areas stated in the single Constitution forced on the various countries that constitute the Nigerian Nation. Obasanjo suspended the allocation and remittance of funds from the federation account to Lagos state.

2001 - The GSM revolution, which was said to have added at least 5% to Nigeria's GDP also happened during Obasanjo's regime. Little or no credit to the government on this though, as it just earned between $200 million and $300 per license from private Nigerian entrepreneurs, who collaborated with foreign partners to build the GSM network. Before the GSM telecoms licenses, there were less than 500,000 phone lines for over 120 million Nigerians at the time.

2005 - Obasanjo was also able to put a team together led by Finance Minister, Ngozi Okonjo-Iweala and head of the newly created Debt Management Office, Mansur Muhtar, to get a debt relief package and help Nigeria exit from the debt trap it was in, due to the corruption and fiscal indiscipline of various military rulers in the past. Over $35 billion was owed mostly to Paris Club creditors by 2004. The relief included both a write-off and buyback of debt.

By 2021, Nigeria was back to a debt trap that was worse than the previous situation where the worry was that debt interest payments were more than capital expenditure. In 2021, debt interest payments have almost matched government revenue, with capital expenditure not even in the conversation. The significant difference (for good and bad reasons) is that the significant portion of the 2021 debt was domestic, which mostly includes the pension assets of workers.

2006 - 2007 - Following disagreements with his Vice President, Atiku Abubakar, Obasanjo surprisingly selects Umaru Musa Yar'Adua, the independent-minded brother of the late Shehu Musa Yar'Adua as his successor, both neutralizing and placating the somewhat formidable camp of the late Yar'Adua with the move.

Obasanjo, a little older, presumably wiser and more experienced than his previous stint as Head of State, still left office with the reputation of 'knowing what to do, but either side-stepping the issue, applying band-aid solutions or leaving the mess for another person to deal with. He failed to address the two of the most obvious forms of corruption in Nigeria, from which the perpetrators earn billions of dollars a year, both from the monetary (forex)and fiscal side (petroleum subsidies) of the economy. Both cases were classic examples of concentrated benefits to the powerful and corrupt, with the dispersed costs borne by the weak, powerless and often uninformed.

Nigeria's import dependent economy means that the demand for forex is almost always more than the supply which is from two main sources, Diaspora remittances and Crude Oil Sales.

The decades long clear and obvious corruption with remittances netted hundreds of millions of dollars to a couple of billions per year (simple arithmetic) for the perpetrators with the Central Bank legitimizing this fraud through the Outward Money Transfer Service. In addition to the ridiculous transfer fees, this cost Diaspora Nigerians and their relatives at home possibly up to a billion dollars most years.[76]

The fact that a 20% - 30% margin has consistently existed for decades between the street and official exchange rates, and that Nigerians in every major city know just where to go meet the 'Aboki' (Hausa word for friend, which is usually the first word uttered by the street money changers) to buy or sell foreign currency shows the scale and primary beneficiaries of the fraud.

There are many angles and aspects of the massive corruption in the Oil industry, but let us focus on a small subsection of the downstream sector with refineries. Nigeria's refineries lose over a billion dollars in most years[77], despite refining almost no products[78]. These losses represent real money from contracts[79], wages etc. for no productivity, which is probably the purest form of corruption you can find This is obvious to anyone with a moderate intelligence, but the National Oil company also has the huge fringe benefit of providing a hidden and shadow treasury for the top echelons of Nigeria's ruling class, and those who believe they own the nation. So, the status quo remains the same when just closing the refineries will save the country these losses (billions) a year, and better still selling them will even bring in some revenue, while saving the country from additional costs of foreign refining and the foreign exchange implications. The jobs and other multiplier effects would have been massive.

In what critics describe as the classic Obasanjo style, he seemed to want to have it both ways, as he was clearly aware of the need for action, but waited till he was leaving office to announce the sale of the refineries[80]. Yar'Adua, perhaps not fully aware of the issues, reversed the sale[81] under pressure from Labor Unions that are sometimes teleguided by the National Oil Company.[82]

By October 2009, Yar'Adua had decided not just to sell the refineries, but stop the National Oil company from participating in the entire downstream sector, in what would have been one of the biggest blows to corruption in Nigeria's history. The National Oil company begged for a month to put things in order before the announcement was made publicly. Yar'Adua never got the opportunity to make that announcement as he was flown out of the country reportedly in a comatose state, within that "extra month."

So Obasanjo left office with no dent to the biggest and most obvious forms and evidence of corruption in Nigerian society, but was happy to introduce useless ineffective and budget draining, role duplicating band aids like the EFCC and ICPC, effectively good for nothing more than hounding political opponents, and forcing the cross carpeting of strategic politicians in areas where whatever 'ruling party' of the day is relatively weak and intends to make inroads.

Olusegun Obasanjo and his successor and PDP flag bearer, Umaru Musa Yar'Adua.

2007 - 2015 Even though Umaru Yar'Adua had never been in the Military, there was still a sense that the Military still cast a long shadow on Nigeria's leadership and politics. Obasanjo's handover to the brother of the late Shehu Musa Yar'Adua, was clearly to spite Atiku but also to compensate for Shehu's death under Abacha. In 2015, former military ruler, Muhammadu Buhari was elected after defeating incumbent President Goodluck Jonathan.

Umaru Musa Yar'adua, Goodluck Jonathan, Muhammadu Buhari

2007 – 2010 - Umaru Musa Yar'Adua's health was a concern for most of his presidency and even before then but he tried to implement some aggressive reforms, famously removing the corrupt subsidy regime on diesel and kerosine and had ordered the removal of the petrol subsidies before he was taken out of Abuja under circumstances that remain questionable.

2009 - A major security development, and some would say resurfacing of structural and foundational issues during the Yar'Adua presidency was the emergence of Boko Haram, led by Muhammed Yusuf and with strong connections to the religious affairs commissioner in Borno state at the time. Since Nigeria was cobbled together (and before actually), there have been a prevalence of individuals and groups claiming legitimacy based on plans to govern society by a purer form of religious rules and edicts, so there was nothing that 'unique' about Boko Haram.

However, following the spate of clashes with the police and other security agencies, which resulted in hundreds of deaths, Boko Haram leader Muhammed Yusuf was arrested by the military and handed over alive to the police. Yusuf would be extrajudicially killed[83] and the group went underground and started an insurgency.

The group and its like-minded religious terrorists soon start a campaign of bombings, initially against churches in the northeast but even in places like Minna, Niger state, but eventually spread take their campaign of terror on all and sundry[84]. Unlike previous times though, including the Maitatsine and various other religious uprisings in the north, the military has been unable to quell the Boko Haram uprising and up to 350,000 people have been killed and millions displaced as of 2020 according to the UNDP.

Mohammed Yusuf and Abubakar Shekau

2010 - In another troubling moment for Nigeria's military, the capital, Abuja is taken over by troops as Yar'Adua is smuggled back into the country in unclear circumstances in which no one was sure whether he was alive or dead. Acting President Goodluck Jonathan was not conferred with, and the capital and villa were placed on lockdown as troops took over the city to return the president to the country. There were fears that a coup was in progress. The president was not seen in public until he was declared and announced as dead on May 5, 2010.[85]

Nigeria's Goodluck?

Goodluck Jonathan's Presidency may be viewed as a time when the influence of the Military (past or present) was not right at the helm of Nigeria's leadership, but it can still be examined from a Military perspective.

Umaru Yar'Adua was unable to officially transmit power to his Vice President, Goodluck Jonathan, as he was taken out of Abuja in unclear circumstances. As the days became weeks and months, with no President, and the Vice President unable to exercise the powers of the President, the country was drifting into an unneeded crisis. This was where Bukola Saraki, Doctor turned politician and chairman of Nigerian Governors forum, stood tall in a uniquely Nigerian brand of statesmanship.

Saraki rallied all the Governors to put pressure on the senators from their States, and a few days later, the Nigerian Senate passed a resolution making Vice President Goodluck Jonathan, the Acting President, through the so-called 'doctrine of necessity,' even without the official transmission of power from the President. There was a price tag, however, and a $4 billion withdrawal from the Excess Crude Account right after Jonathan assumed Presidential powers, only turned out to be an initial down-payment.

The Excess Crude Account (ECA) was a simple, yet effective mechanism to save the extra earnings from Oil proceeds over the Budgeted or Benchmark crude price for the year. However, there wasn't much in terms of safeguarding the monies saved, outside of a President's will and resistance (typical Obasanjo half measure, some would say). Smelling blood, the Governors demanded more[86], and in just a few months, the savings to the ECA stalled as withdrawals became regular, and the account quietly transitioned from savings to a current account[87]

This subtle but clear shift to the Governors as the fulcrum of political power was a key factor of Jonathan's eventual 5-year Presidency, but first there was the curious matter of James Ibori, who along with Saraki helped influence the emergence of Jonathan as Yar'Adua's Vice-President.

Ibori (with Umaru Yar'Adua) and Saraki (with Jonathan and Sambo) were foiled in their quest to be the new 'Capos' of Nigerian Politics.

While the Ibori-Saraki support for Jonathan had as much to do with neutralizing Peter Odili's path to the Vice Presidency (and to a lesser extent, Donald Duke's), the speed with which Jonathan turned on Ibori surprised most, and after a failed attempt to arrest him (Ibori) at Oghara[88], he slipped out of the country. He was eventually arrested in Dubai and extradited to England, where he was jailed on corruption charges.

Ibori, had somehow left himself exposed by not joining the Nigerian senate, which is the standard move of most ex-governors in Nigeria. Perhaps he assumed his role in the emergence of Yar'Adua and Jonathan would guarantee his protection. It did, while Yar'Adua was alive and well. Saraki would not repeat Ibori's mistake and promptly ended up in the Nigerian senate upon completing his 2nd term as Governor of Kwara State.

Goodluck Jonathan undertook a number of other ultimately unwise political battles. Perhaps this was to curtail the growing influence of the Governors, or maybe it was to grow his own political base. These would later prove quite costly, but first of all there was the 'Banana Peel' of the 2011 election.

Hardliners like Lawal Kaita[89] threatened to make Nigeria ungovernable for Jonathan if he contested the 2011 elections, while other politicians like Adamu Ciroma asked him to respect the PDP's rotational Presidency agreement and not seek the party nomination.[90]

Widespread cases of underage voting have been reported in Nigeria's far North.

Despite these threats, Goodluck Jonathan defeated Buhari as expected in 2011. The reactions to the election exposed another dark and bitter aspect in Nigeria's history and politics. Spontaneous violence broke out in Nigeria's far North as the results were announced. At least 10 Youth Corpers from the 'South' and 'Middle Belt' were among the up to 100 people[91] murdered as senseless violence broke out over elections that Buhari definitely had no chance of winning.

It is normal to have Corpers assist the electoral commission with administrative and field functions during elections in Nigeria, and despite widespread criticism on the continuation of the Youth Service scheme in its current form, 'Corpers' are generally seen as 'other peoples' children that should be protected, wherever they are in the country. The killing of male and female corpers over elections where Buhari's supporters were proven to be involved in massive acts of rigging and underage voting, was a new low in the already depressing history of Nigeria.

The murdered Corpers included Chibuzor Ukeoma, Jehleel Adeniji, Tosin Teidi, Chukwuonyerem Nwazema, Seun Adewunmi, Obinna Okpokiri, Sule Akonyi, Elliot Adowei and Ayotunde Gbenjo.

Jonathan hosted the families and promised to bring the culprits to book. He donated N5 million (about $25,000 at the time) to each family and promised automatic employment to someone from each bereaved family. [92]

The father of one of the slain Corpers, Mr. Awuchewu Okpokiri, captured the mood of most reasonable and peace-loving people, when he observed that "communication in the last violence was nothing to write home about. A lot of us did not know (about) the death of these children until April 24 for something that happened on April 18. We also want to ask just like every other Nigerian is saying today that the NYSC scheme should be reviewed in all its ramifications."

There was no record of any commiseration with the families or regret over the killings by Candidate Buhari. Rather, he seemed to threaten more bloodshed with a troubling statement concerning the next elections about a year later that 'Dogs and Baboons will be soaked in blood'[93].

It is also not known if the Jonathan administration fulfilled its promises to the families of the slain corpers, outside of the monies paid, as 10 years later (2021), Sunday Dare, Buhari's Minister overseeing the NYSC scheme re-announced the employment of the family members as announced a decade earlier.[94]

Youth Corpers on electoral duty: At least 10 Corpers were hunted down and killed in the communities where they were

posted to and served, as INEC announced the result of elections Candidate Buhari had no shot of winning.

The widespread violence that followed the 2011 election was insightful in a few ways. The first was that support for Buhari, even though very much in the minority across the Nation, was significant in Hausa Country. The CPC candidate, given his past record of incompetence, was seen as some sort of comic relief, each electoral campaign cycle. Statements credited to him, which suggested increasing support and defense of terrorism and extremism also meant that there was no way he could be accepted into the mainstream of Nigerian politics, even in its broken state on his sectional CPC platform.

However, the millions of out of school and itinerant (Almajiri) kids in Hausa and Kanuri Country would soon grow and have voter's cards and be a voting base. Hundreds of thousands, and possibly millions of them, already voted in past elections anyway.

Former Lagos Governor, **Bola Tinubu** pondered on these facts, and saw a window of opportunity. His limited, but well-funded Action Congress of Nigeria controlled Lagos, and occasionally, some surrounding states. It was a long shot, but still a window; and Jonathan, with his unwise political battles, would help expand that window.

Goodluck Jonathan was meant to be the one that was different. The one who came from nowhere and somehow made its right to the top due to a number of extraordinary events that catapulted him to the leadership of the Nigerian State.

Before Yar'Adua's death and Ibori/Saraki influencing Obasanjo to get him the Vice Presidency, he was Deputy Governor of the Ijaw heartland state of Bayelsa, but the Governor, retired Air Force Squadron Leader Diepreye Alamieyeseigha was impeached, leading to a relatively short tenure for Goodluck as Governor of Bayelsa before becoming Nigeria's Vice President.

Alamieyeseigha reportedly selected Jonathan as Deputy Governor for the same reason Ibori and Saraki wanted him as Vice President, someone who ticked some checkmarks, but would pose no threat or resistance to his or their own plans and schemes. His 'real-world' experience was reportedly largely limited to OMPADEC, the predecessor institution to the Niger-Delta Development Commission, before politics found him.

There was a feel-good story about Goodluck Jonathan. A genuine outsider from the Niger-Delta region that had borne the environmental and sometimes oppressive burden of producing the oil that had been one of the weak glues binding the Nigerian State over most of its post-independence decades. He was not part of the political or economic elite and often told of how he grew up so poor that he could not afford a pair of shoes (hence the "Goody no shoes" nickname). There were hopes that his own background and outsider status would translate to massive improvements in a lot of the tens of millions of the extremely poor in the country.

However, the lack of experience, indecisiveness, and a tendency to take on needless political battles were a huge constraint on his administration and would cost him severely.

His 'war' on Rivers Governor Chibuike Rotimi Amaechi was a clear example. The root cause of the issues is the subject of some speculation. It could have been:

1) To loosen the hold of the Governors that ran Jonathan ragged during his first months as Acting President, and later President. Amaechi took over from Saraki as Chairman of the Governor's forum.

2) Due to Jonathan taking sides in an internal State battle between Amaechi and Nyesom Wike, Amaechi's former Chief of Staff, who was later Jonathan's Minister of State for Education. Seizing control of Rivers' politics tends to be violent, even by Nigerian standards (hence the unpleasant nickname 'Rivers of Blood,' and soon the State Governor was being hounded and harassed within[95] and outside his base [96] by 'Abuja power'[97]

3) Possibly due to a reported clash between Amaechi and Jonathan's wife and first lady, Patience Jonathan, a Rivers State indigene. Demolitions, Urban redevelopment, contracts and other stated reasons did not seem serious enough for the very messy and public skirmishes. Goodluck Jonathan himself suggested that this was the real problem.[58]

Jonathan's failure or oversight in reconciling the warring factions in Rivers (sadly, it always boils down to sharing political office and access to the treasury, as the departing Governor usually wants to install a stooge and go to the Senate) meant that Amaechi was feeling isolated within the ruling party, and became a prime target for the previously fragmented, but suddenly consolidating opposition.

Jonathan then stalled on implementing decisions that Yar'Adua had taken to end corruption in the downstream petroleum sector, perhaps with an eye on the 2011 Presidential election. That was no excuse however, for his hilarious decision to put the fox in charge of the hen house and have the

NNPC lead a supposed deregulation of the downstream sector that did not involve the removal of critical downstream sector assets including the pipelines and refineries from the control of NNPC and its subsidiaries, but seemed to zone in on Price increases and subsidy removal. The NNPC-Labor Union collaboration was in full swing once again with street protests, some of which were headlined by ignorant and misguided opposition figures. The President quickly ended the half-hearted process in January 2012.

A comprehensive reform in the downstream sector would have given Jonathan his signature economic achievement. Obasanjo could point to the jump in GDP from mobile phones (again the Government did almost nothing, but earn license fees here), clearing the external debt, and getting the military firmly out of the political space, even though he side-stepped a clear constitutional violation like Sharia. Implementing Yar'Adua's downstream sector reforms could have been a major boost to the economy in terms of jobs, income from sales and concession of downstream assets, forex savings (no more importation of refined product necessary) and possibly earnings, a boost in Government revenue due to the end of fraudulent deductions by NNPC, and if combined with forex reforms, would have definitely led to cheaper petroleum products regardless of the global crude prices or the exchange rate.

The reversal of the downstream sector reforms was not the only time that Jonathan changed his mind on critical and non-critical policy issues. He was famous for doing that. The University of Lagos (UNILAG) became Moshood Abiola

University (MAULAG) and following protests, quickly transformed back to UNILAG.

With the selection of Pre-Shipment Inspectors for crude oil exports, a Ministry of Finance panel had shortlisted four companies based on the pre-set criteria from the State House/ President's Office and concluded the process. A few months later, names of 11 companies were sent back with the suggestion that the process be redone. Eventually, all 11 were selected as Crude export Pre-shipment inspectors, with the contracts renewed as the President was about to leave office.[99] A badly run orphanage with good, well intentioned people has a high probability of doing major damage and hurting the children, and a well and efficiently run criminal organization may be useful, under the right combination of close monitoring, risk management and threat of sanctions, as was the case with Lucky Luciano and the US Navy in World War II.

The scale of miscues from Jonathan's office during his Presidency suggests a poorly run State House, and the blame must naturally go to his Chief of Staff. There were suggestions that Jonathan struck up a friendship with Oghiadomhe and chose him as his most important aide, based on their similar experiences as 'long-suffering' deputies to Governors, with Oghiadomhe serving as a two-term deputy Governor to Lucky Igbinedion in Edo State.

The President's relative lack of experience, and possibly knowledge about the Nigerian State needed a strong office that would strengthen and guide, and not weaken the President. The key and relevant factors had to be considered before decisions were made. The number of decision reversals on even relatively simple issues suggest that the office did not provide the much needed support to the required level. Oghi-adomhe was eventually replaced in 2014, but it was probably a little too late at the time.

Jonathan was still favored to win the election, but the opposition was no longer made up of fragmented units led by extremists and local champions who could be dismissed with a wave of the hand.

2010 - Goodluck Jonathan appoints Azubuike Ihejirika as Chief of Army Staff. Nigeria's first Igbo Army Chief since the end of the Nigeria-Biafra Civil War.

Madueke, First Igbo service Chief, and Ihejirika - first Igbo Army since the end of the Nigeria-Biafra Civil War.

2011 - Boko Haram attacks the UN building in Abuja, Nigeria's Capital, killing 21 and injuring several others. The attack on a high-profile civilian target in the center of the country, showed a worrying dimension to the group's strategy and capacity. This new dimension to the group's terrorism is repeated, when another soft civilian target far away from its Kanuri country base is attacked on Christmas day. 37 people were killed and several others injured in the attack on St.

Theresa's Catholic Church in Madalla, just outside Abuja. Abaji based religious teacher (with up to 500 kids reportedly under his tutelage), Kabiru Umar Dikko (aka Kabiru Sokoto) is arrested, tried and convicted for the Madalla terrorist attack.

The arrest of Sokoto, a non-Kanuri, with no links or history to Kanuri Country questioned the narrative that Boko-Haram was largely a Kanuri affair, with some Hausa minority involvement. [100]

Top Left - Interior of the UN Building; Top Right - Exterior of St. Theresa's Catholic Church; Bottom- Kabiru (Sokoto) Umar Dikko at trial.

2012 - Former National Security Adviser Owoye Andrew Azazi (a former Army and Defense Chief) died in a naval helicopter crash alongside Patrick Yakowa. Azazi had been recently sacked by Jonathan under immense pressure from 'The North' (euphemism for the Foreign Fuduyan Fulbe factor in Nigeria), While Jonathan suggested that 'consultations with foreign leaders' made him fire Azazi, a leading newspaper seemed more in tune with what most of the public knew.

Traditionally, the North considers the position of NSA as its own. People from the zone had constantly been appointed the NSA until Jonathan summoned the courage to appoint Azazi following the resignation of Aliyu Gusau, who also vied for the presidential ticket of the PDP with Jonathan in 2011. While Jonathan was said to have rebuffed all attempts from the North to recover the seat since he appointed Azazi, the continued bombings and atmosphere of insecurity that pervaded the country were said to have made him to change his mind. [101]

Azazi was replaced by Sambo Dasuki, IBB's first ADC while he was Military ruler, and also the son of the former top Fulbe clan leader in Nigeria.

Kaduna Governor, Patrick Yakowa, and former National Security Adviser, Patrick Azazi died in a helicopter crash.

2014 - Boko Haram gained international attention with the kidnapping of hundreds of schoolgirls from Chibok, a minority village on the fringes of Kanuri Country in Borno State. Often ignored or underreported was the fact that this terrorist group had also killed dozens of schoolboys in Yobe state, shortly before the kidnap of the girls in Chibok. Goodluck Jonathan seemed to assume an unnecessary catch-22 stance of 'damned-if-you-do-damned-if-you-don't'; And for a while, he didn't, as the government was slow to react or take action on the mass killings (in Yobe) and kidnappings (in Chibok) of secondary school children.

Part of Jonathan's challenge was the sharp criticism he faced when attempting to ramp up action on Boko Haram. Most of these came from 'Northern' (i.e., mostly Hausaland's Fulbe elite) leaders including serial candidate Buhari who reasoned that 'attacks on Boko Haram were attacks on the North'[102] Goodluck Jonathan seemed overwhelmed, and sometimes unsure and indecisive. A big reason for this was the level of support he received from his office for most of his administration. However, as the leader he bears ultimate responsibility for not identifying weaknesses quickly and making necessary changes.

Chibok girls held captive by Boko Haram terrorists.

Some have suggested that the 'Niger-Delta' has blown its chance at 'leadership' since Jonathan did not represent the 'Zone' well. This is hilarious, if not outrightly ridiculous, for a number of reasons:

- The Niger-Delta has several capable leaders and achievers, but like most 'normal and responsible' Nigerians, they stay away from the criminal reality show and minefield of Nigerian Politics.
- If the ethnic groups and countries in the region decide to band together and demand the permanent Presidency of a Nigerian state that has been largely funded and sustained by the oil fortuitously located on their lands and waterways, it is worthy of consideration and negotiation, especially since there has been nothing for-

tuitous about the environmental damage suffered by the region due to the negligence of forces and people that are mostly external to the region. It is up to the other funders of the Nigerian State (Customs Duty, Corporate Income and Value Added Tax providers) to make their demands on the tune they want played for paying the piper.

- Goodluck Jonathan was not chosen by the 'Niger-Delta,' as Obasanjo, Ibori and Saraki, and a few others who handpicked Jonathan as Yar'Adua's running mate were not representing the region with their actions.
- Corruption is definitely a cancer, and cases of corruption under Jonathan or any other leader will not be justified or excused. However, the sensational cases of corruption reported under Jonathan, headlined by the billions of dollars of missing revenue calculated from the gap between expected revenue from crude sales and remitted revenue by NNPC have continued in the administration of his successor without a whimper from the Central Bankers, past or current (as at 2021). Specific cases of individual corruption that have been reported are also just as bad, if not worse, given the impact and outcomes (crazy government borrowing, accelerated exchange rate depreciation etc.).
  - It is difficult for a device to act differently from what it was created to perform and it is virtually impossible to construct a certain type of building when the foundation was designed for another. Nigeria was conceived in corruption, exists for corruption, and operates by corruption. As such

the end result and outcomes can only be corruption. It should be noted that the planners, executioners and beneficiaries of the corrupt Nigerian state are almost exclusively foreigners with no longstanding cultural and historical ties to the indigenous peoples and countries that are wholly or partly trapped in the Nigerian State. This is also why this book will waste little time with corruption taxonomies and catalogues.

Frontpage of leading Newspaper 'Vanguard' announced the defection of Amaechi and the newPDP Governors to APC

2015 - Unresolved security challenges and concerns over unchecked corruption contributed to the defeat of Goodluck Jonathan in the 2015 election. Interestingly, these issues have arguably increased under the Buhari administration. What really did Jonathan in however, was the cannibalization of his own (potential, if not active) electoral asset base, which almost directly led to a strengthening of the opposition. Former Lagos Governor, Tinubu had orchestrated a merger of "strange bedfellows" between his ACN and Buhari's CPC, but even that was unlikely to knock off the ruling party without the New PDP (5 Governors that defected from the ruling party to the new coalition), Saraki, and crucially Amaechi, who served as the Director-General of both of Buhari's successful runs at Nigeria's Presidency.

Amaechi, Tinubu and Buhari
2015 - Buhari quickly appoints a GMD for the National Oil company, NNPC, but waits for almost 6 months after his

inauguration before announcing a cabinet, famously saying that Ministers are 'Noisemakers'[103]. This must have sounded like a lottery cashout for leading civil servants, for obvious reasons.

2015 - Buhari's personally retains Petroleum Ministry portfolio[104] and his faction of the winning 'coalition' naturally gets the lion share of his appointments, to the boundary of obvious nepotism[105], according to some. However, coalition members, and rumored election sponsors, Tinubu and Amaechi, seem to be well 'taken care of,' with Tinubu's camp providing Buhari's Vice President, Yemi Osinbajo amongst other positions, and Amaechi personally taking the portfolios of Transport and Aviation.

Saraki seems out in the cold, but not for long, as he orchestrates a 'coup' in the Senate, and becomes Senate President, with the help of opposition PDP Senators. A similar move in the 2nd arm of the legislature, the House of Representative sees Yakubu Dogara emerge as speaker. Both moves secure victories over the ruling party candidates for the positions.

Dogara with Saraki

2015 - A convoy of the Army Chief, Lt. Gen Tukur Buratai is held up in a Zaria neighborhood by Shiite (Shia, also sometimes referred to as Islamic Movement of Nigeria (IMN)) Youth. The Youth were supposedly protesting an earlier incident where members of the group were reportedly attacked by soldiers. Shiite - Army Clashes had occurred over the past year, following a clash during the group's procession that reportedly resulted in the death of the sons of the leader, Ibrahim Zakzaky.

A couple of senior officers in the convoy got down to reason with the youth, many of whom were armed with stones and sticks from the images seen from the incident. Machetes/ Cutlasses were also reported. Over the next 24 hours, members of the group mobilized to the compound of the leader to prevent his arrest, which was suspected, but not announced.

Things quickly escalated and over the next few days, about 350 members of the group were killed, according to reliable accounts, which also reported that Zakzaky and his wife, Zeenah were injured and arrested.[107]

Senior Army Officers in the Chief of Army Staff's convoy try to appeal to and negotiate with IMN Youth for 'passage rights.'

Zakzaky, as an Economics major and students' religious leader/activist in the 70's was impressed by the Khomeini revolution in Iran, and soon started a Shia movement in Northern Nigeria, after spending some time in Iran.

The IMN soon became a noticeable even if small minority group, and even though the group has an objective to create an Islamic State in Nigeria, it is not known to have taken up an armed struggle against existing religious, traditional and political institutions. It is also not known to have killed indigenous peoples or taken their lands. This is a contrast from the Foreign Fuduyan Fulbe takeover of Hausaland or the dozens of similarly minded individuals and groups that have attempted to introduce their own brand of religious regime since.

Quite naturally, the growth of the IMN led to a proxy war between Iran and Saudi Arabia, and Senior Saudi Royals 'reportedly boasted of Riyadh's success in the suppression of El-Zakzaky'[108] with respect to the Zaria incident and the Group's travails, according to IMN Spokesman Abdullahi Mohammed

While a proxy war between Iran and Saudi Arabia is not unexpected, there is an interesting and very local dimension to Zakzaky's troubles with the Fulbe rulers of Hausaland. The Fuduyan takeover of Hausaland was by foreigners, who identify and can easily be identified as such. The takeover has remained effective for two centuries as the foreign clans maintained a stronghold over the traditional, religious and political institutions and symbols of authority in Hausa Country.

Zakzaky represents a small (as at 2021) but genuine threat to that stronghold. An indigenous and alternative symbol of religious authority. He is not claiming to be Arab or Saudi, just a Hausa religious leader.

While an overwhelming majority of Hausas are still subject to the Wahabbi aligned Fulbe religious authorities, the thought of an alternative, fully indigenous religious authority and institution in Hausaland is extremely discomforting to the ruling clans.

It was definitely not surprising that there would be a major incident as soon as Buhari became Nigeria's President. Buhari had always seemed eager to prove his 'Fulbeness' to the ruling clans, given his Mother's Kanuri background and his somewhat lower origins in their ranking system. He was reportedly born in a camp of migrating Fulbes along the current Niger - Nigerian border, and many have used this to highlight that he has no cultural, ethnic and historical ties to any indigenous Nigerian groups. The Fulbe 'cabal' supposedly led by Buhari's older nephew Mamman Daura (who lived in the Presidential Villa complex during Buhari's presidency) seemed to have milked this 'desire to belong' extensively.

A strange twist to this, is that Buhari also sees himself as some sort of living armistice to the centuries' long war between the Fuduyan Fulbes and the Kanuris. Fuduye and Mohammed Bello, having killed off or deposed the rulers of Hausaland, turned their attention to the Kanuris (Kanem-Borno), Hausaland's eastern neighbors. El-Kanemi, the Kanuri leader, was better prepared than the Hausa rulers though, as the Kanuris have had to move base and capital over time due to various armed adventurists with religious claims trying to take over their country before and after the Fuduyans. Some of the more famous among these were the Sudanese Rabih-az-Zubayr and the more recent Boko-Haram insurgents.

Buhari seemed to pull both groups (one foreign, the other, only partially on Nigeria's Northeastern Fringes[109]) into a strong ruling alliance that goes far beyond a kitchen cabinet[110]. That sadly, is the reality of the Nigerian State cobbled together by foreigners and run for the benefit of foreigners. One where the capacity of indigenous peoples and countries to function, cater to their welfare, and defend themselves has been taken away. One where foreign militia and terrorists roam the country seemingly unchallenged, sacking villages and taking land[111], while attempts by local people to defend themselves and chase the terrorist away are suppressed by a Military that amazingly somehow uses the insignia that the Foreign Fuduyan Fulbes used while taking over Hausa country.

2018 - Alex Badeh, former Chief of Air Staff and Chief of Defense Staff is gunned down in the suburbs of Abuja despite the presence of his security team.

2018 - With Buhari conveniently out of the country and power "legally transmitted" to his Vice President, the long awaited move against Saraki happens (there had been several 'minor' EFCC arraignments, and a ridiculous link to a major armed robbery in Offa) with the secret police (DSS) sealing off the National Assembly for reasons that officially remain unclear[112]. The move, which immediately draws widespread condemnation, is reportedly as much of a surprise to the public as it is to the Vice President, Yemi Osinbajo, who immediately summoned Lawal Daura, head of the secret service agency.

Daura reportedly condescendingly reminds Osinbajo of his political irrelevance in the scheme of things, and Osinbajo, said to be unable to reach Buhari announces the suspension of Daura, and replaces him with Matthew Seiyefa, in an acting capacity.

The move by Osinbajo, his most aggressive as Vice President, met with almost instant repercussion. Seiyefa was promptly replaced with Yusuf Bichi[113], and Finance Minister, Kemi Adeosun, one of Osinbajo's two Ministerial appointees in his role as coordinator of the economy, resigns under circumstances pertaining to her exemption certificate from the National Youth Service. The other 'Osinbajo' Minister, Okey

Enelamah, a Private Equity executive in charge of the Trade, Investment and Industry Portfolio is not retained, as Buhari is re-elected in 2019.

R-L Buhari, Saraki and former Central Bank Governor Lamido Sanusi

2019 - Former Babangida ADC, Jonathan's National Security Adviser and son of former Fuduyan Fulbe clan leader, Sambo Dasuki, in detention despite several prior court orders granting him bail, is released alongside activist and Sahara Reporter's publisher, Omoyele Sowore. Dasuki is alleged to have 'shared' $2billion meant for Arms procurement to various political associates,[114] but his troubles may have been compounded due to Buhari's long-standing grudge over his (Dasuki) role in the IBB coup.

Sowore's release seems to have been due to some US pressure[115], with Dasuki thrown into the mix to 'equalize' things. However, still illegally detained by Buhari was Shiite leader, Ibrahim El-Zakzaky, who is seen as a risk to Nigeria's ruling Fulbe class that controls the religious, traditional, and government institutions in Hausa land.

Zakzaky was released in 2021, as the Buhari Government prepared for the (separate) trials of IPOB leader Nnamdi Kanu and Sunday Igboho, who escalated his protests of Fulbe herdsmen killings to rallies and demands for a separate Afeire Nation.

Dasuki, El-Zakzaky and Sowore

2019 - In a brazen, unlawful and almost unprecedented move[116], Buhari removes the Chief Justice of the Country, Walter Onnoghen, in the build up to the 2019 elections.[117] The move is seen as ensuring that there would be no surprise through the courts, as Buhari prepared to square up against Atiku Abubakar in the elections. Buhari termed the removal as a suspension to bypass the requirement of getting two-thirds of the senate of sanctioning the move.

2019 - Unsurprisingly, Muhammadu Buhari, whose rule as Military dictator left the Nigerian economy in shambles, and who did not even seem to be interested in attempting to fulfill his electoral promises during his first term as civilian ruler[118], is re-elected as President, a development that some discerning minds believe to be the countdown to the death knell of the clearly failing Nigerian State[119]. Buhari, is, however, extremely popular in the far north of the country even though his image had been carefully managed by an extensive media network, starting from his older nephew, Mamman Daura, who was editor of the conservative New Nigerian newspaper between 1969 and 1975. His inner circle also includes Isa Funtua, a past President of the Newspapers Proprietors Association of Nigeria, and Abba Kyari, who worked with Daura at New Nigerian, and was Buhari's first Chief of Staff. It was no surprise that an organization with scores of staff called the Buhari Media Organization, was set up to launder Buhari's image, and counter any stories, true or not, considered not to favor the public image that had been built up.

2021 - Former military officer, doctor and self-appointed negotiator and spokesman of terrorists, Ahmad Abubakar Gumi (Jr), blatantly lied in a meeting with terrorists (aka bandits) that non-Moslem soldiers were attacking Moslem communities, attempting to create a division and break the camaraderie of officers serving in the military. Nothing mentioned about the high school student killed in cold blood as the terrorists kidnapped the victims.

The Government appeared to back Gumi in statements that seemed incomprehensible to sane, rational minds. False rumors of Gumi Jr's invitation by the military and intelligence agencies were later denied[120].

A few days after Gumi's remarks and meeting with the terrorists in Niger state, a Beechcraft 3501 surveillance aircraft that was involved in the search for the kidnapped Niger state schoolboys, with a seven-man crew, surprisingly all non-Moslem, in a very religiously diverse Nigerian Military, crashed shortly after a refueling stop at the Abuja airport. While the official report of the crash has not been released, foul play or sabotage has not been ruled out, given Gumi Jr's comments, the timing of the crash, and the identity of the victims.

Images from an official Military announcement of the transition of the Officers and Men killed on a mission trying to locate the position of the terrorists that kidnapped Students in

Niger State in February 2021. Perhaps an invitation of Gumi Jr by even one of several budget consuming agencies (Police, DSS, DMI, NSA, NIA etc.) would have confirmed the location of the terrorists, making the surveillance flight unnecessary.

2021 - Chief of Army Staff, Lt. Gen Ibrahim Attahiru, and 10 other officers and men of the military died in another Beechcraft 3501 Aircraft crash, this time, as the plane attempted to land in bad weather, and was redirected to the civilian Airport in Kaduna[121]. The Army Chief had only been in office for a few months, and was going to attend a military graduation ceremony.

Public information about military crash inquiries is hard to come by in Nigeria, so additional details regarding the cause of the crash may be unknown for some time, outside of 'inclement weather conditions' at the time, which may, or may not have been a major determinant.

2021 - President Buhari departs the country for London in late July for a postponed[122] Medical trip that now includes an education donors conference. Bola Tinubu is curiously in London at the same time, so a 'state of the alliance talks' may also be on the unannounced agenda. Despite vowing to oppose medical tourism if elected as President during his campaign[123], Buhari had spent over 200 days on medical trips[124] to London as at 2021, with his wife, Aisha, suggesting that the Buhari Government did not have the competence to ensure the Presidential Villa Clinic was properly run and adequately stocked with the most basic medication, including syringes[125].

London has been a choice meeting point for Buhari and Tinubu over the years.

2021 - Terrorist attacks and kidnappings continue in many parts of the country, with Southern Kaduna and Plateau remaining among the key flashpoints. In Kaduna, 13 schools, mostly run by religious organizations are closed following the kidnapping of scores of students from Baptist High School[126]. In the neighboring Jos Plateau indigenes accuse the GOC of one of the Army's major divisions of being on an "evil mission to ... wipe out the chiefdom ' since the marauders attack in broad daylight, steal, kill, rape and destroy farmlands."[127] Those fears followed complaints about what seemed to be a pattern of the Army not intervening when foreign Fulbes (based on eyewitness accounts) attack communities with high grade weapons, but eagerly intervene when communities rally to go after the killers.

Many wonder why the Nigerian Army still retains the insignia from the flag of an invading foreign Fulbe militia, as it took over Hausa Country, and if this this signals the ideological and spiritual purpose of the Nigerian Army, and the Nation it helped forge, and has struggled (rightly or wrongly) to keep together.

A cartoon in the Punch, a leading newspaper, captures the widely held thought by indigenous Nigerians on the stance of the Military regarding invading foreign terrorists.

In what seemed to be an exclamation mark on the security situation (even if calling it that is diversionary), two commissioned officers were killed by terrorists, and a third kidnapped from the Officers' Quarters of the Nigerian Defense Academy (think of West Point, USAFA and the Naval Academy all rolled into one). It was symbolic and ironic that the entire Military was covered in this attack, as the Officers were from the three Armed Forces with Major Christopher Datong

(Army) abducted, and Lt. Cdr Wulah (Navy) and Flt Lt Oko-ronkwo (Air Force) killed.

On the same night (or the next) as the NDA attack, about a four-hour drive to the Southeast, terrorists killed over 30 in-digenes in their homes[128], following widely expected attacks that had seen evacuations of non-Indigenes from the University of Jos.[129]

In the Jos attacks, and in previous attacks around the NDA vicinity[130], foreign Fulbe Militia, or Bandits, as the Herdsmen without cattle are now called, were confirmed by victims[131] to be their attackers and abductors[132].

Nigeria does not have a security problem per se. It has a structural problem, and an invasion problem. This can be resolved easily by the constituent countries picking up the gauntlet and functioning as countries to protect life and prop-erty.

The military and the police cannot even protect itself from the raving militia of foreign invaders but are quick to kill in-digenes trying to protect their lives and lands. Every country in the Nigerian nation is sustainable at levels far above subsis-tence. The priority of each country MUST be the protection of the lives, lands and livelihoods of its indigenes and legal res-idents.

Fulbes are indigenous to at least six nations of their own in West Africa and face no natural or manmade threats in these countries, which are not contiguous to the Nigerian State. Fulbe's are also at the political helm in most of these coun-tries. The Fulbes passing through or residing in Nigeria, es-pecially the ruling clans of Hausaland, know where they are from, and have close ties with their home countries. That is why Fulbe Cleric, Dahiru Bauchi will, from his people, marry the daughter of *Senegalese* Cleric, Ibrahim Inyass. Similarly, Aisha Buhari's Chief Guest at her son's Wedding activities was the wife of *Gambian* Fulbe President Adama Barrow.

Perhaps the only difference is that the Fulbe ruling clans of Hausaland believe that they must maintain an extremist and intolerant religious stance for a public show of control and claim to credibility (For instance, Umar Tall stayed with Mohammed Bello in Sokoto for years, to gain practical lessons in 'how to invade and destroy previously sustainable societies', although his attempts in their homelands had mixed res). On a related note, the clans naturally believe in using the wealth and influence of the 'Nigerian Countries' to exert influence and achieve their objectives in their home countries.

Aisha Buhari and her Fulbe Guests from Home.

The lives of the millions of indigenous Nigerians cannot be mortgaged to ruling rights of the Fulbe ruling clans of Hausa Country, and the plundering and killing 'rights' of Bandits, Herdsmen, Militia, or whatever other label with which the terrorists are tagged.

2021 - The Nigerian government banned the use of the global social media platform, Twitter, in the Nation. Twitter had deleted comments from President Buhari's verified account, which suggested that the unrest in the Southeastern region (Ndigbo country) could reignite the civil war.

The ban lasted for 7 months (June 2021-January 2022) and was lifted as both sides agreed on face saving conditions, with Twitter establishing a legal subsidiary within Nigeria and promising to prevent or limit the use of the platform for misinformation and fake news.

2021 - Nnamdi Kanu, leader of the Indigenous People of Biafra (IPOB) is arrested in Kenya and flown back to Nigeria. Sources close to Kanu suggest that he was kidnapped, but it is unlikely that Nigerian agents operated without the knowledge and cooperation of Kenyan authorities, similar to what the Turkish and Israeli government did to capture Abdullah Ocalan, the Kurdish separatist leader, in Nairobi, two decades earlier. Like Ocallan, Kanu was bundled into a waiting private jet and flown out of Kenya.

The arrest of Kanu fails to break the tension and stalemate in the 'Ndigbo' states, as the bank on work, movement and market activities on Mondays remains effective.

2022 - Terrorists breached a train on the popular Abuja - Kaduna service with bombs and gunfire, killing 8 passengers and kidnaping over 60 passengers. The service had become popular following the frequent kidnapping on the road linking the two cities. Many high profile passengers, including the CEO of a government owned bank were among the kidnapped. Among the killed were young professionals including a medical doctor.

Nigeria's Statistics agency estimates that $1.44 billion (N2.3 trillion) was paid in ransom to kidnappers in the 12 months ending April 2024[133].

2021 - 2023 - The attempt by the Nigeria based Fuduyan Fulbe hegemony to wrestle power from Alpha Conde in their Guinean homeland may have helped to trigger a string of coups across West and Central Africa and splinter ECOWAS.

Following Conde's refusal of entreaties to ease the stage for a Fulbe President in Guinea, and his controversial victory in the ensuing election, rival candidate Cellou candidate, backed by Nigeria's Fulbe hegemony and Guinea Bissau's Embolo[134], refused to concede and declared himself President[135]. Political chaos often gives room for military adventurism, and Mamadou Doumbouya, head of Conde's Special Forces Group, took over the Government.

A few months later, Doumbouya's Malian pal from a joint US training session a few years back, took over the government in Mali. Coups in Burkina Faso and Niger soon followed, as did one in Gabon. However, the Coup in Niger had the most significant impact on Nigeria, and together with the Coups in Mali and Burkina Faso, eventually splintered ECOWAS.

2023 - The Central Bank's decision to change the currency print and colors result in a massive and widespread shortage of currency. In what is perhaps a uniquely Nigerian situation, the naira currency was trading at a premium to itself (or its value), as high as 30% in some instances. This problem would endure for at least 2 years, with street hawkers, party money changers, and even bank managers getting in on the act[136].

2023 - Bola Tinubu wins the 2023 Presidential election by getting 37% of the votes cast in an election in which the participation rate was 27%, thereby getting the mandate with less than 10% of the 90 million eligible votes. Other major candidates were former Vice President Atiku Abubakar of the PDP, former Anambra Governor and Atiku's running mate four years earlier, Peter Obi, and former Kano Governor, Rabiu Musa Kwankwaso.

Peter Obi had pulled a shocker by decamping from the main opposition PDP, and joining the Labor Party, just before the PDP Presidential primaries. He picked the Labor Party ticket and powered to 3rd place with over 6 million votes in the main election, winning in Lagos, Abuja and with a dominant majority in all the Southeast states. Kwankwaso won in his core base of Kano, while Tinubu and Atiku had favorable results from various parts of the Nation[137].

2023 - Bola Tinubu announces the removal of fuel subsidies during his inauguration speech; a bold, positive, and commendable move. He however falters on the clear and set guidelines and pathways for the all-encompassing reforms in Nigeria's downstream sector by strengthening (not ending) NNPC's participation in Nigeria's downstream sector. The government also fails in its strategy for the needed forex reforms by failing to connect its fiscal and monetary policy, incapacitating itself from the ability to use a key monetary tool (forex allocation) to drive positive fiscal change and behavior (corporate taxes).

The strange decision by the government to maintain a stronghold and presence where it is not needed (downstream petroleum sector), and abdicate responsibility in a forex market where a very limited presence could be hugely catalytic for fiscal impact leads to suggestions of foul play and 'state capture' by various parties, including Aliko Dangote, who suggested that NNPC officials had blending plants in Malta[138] and were determined to continue the official importation of refined petroleum products.[139] The uniformity of prices and official importation means that the 'subsidy' is transferred from the Government to the NNPC, which can keep declaring the differential between the landing costs (it sets) and market price of Petroleum products as operational losses.

The NNPC also struggles to supply the Dangote refinery with the Crude it needs to operate the refinery, which has more than enough capacity to supply the local market, making Dangote source Crude Oil from International markets.

As expected, and predicted in the first volume of this series, Nigeria's national oil company will not let go of its multibillion-dollar freebies, which is rooted in the inefficiency and corruption it oversees in Nigeria's petroleum industry. Despite enough capacity to fully refine its local petroleum needs, Nigeria was still massively importing petroleum products, while starving a domestic refinery, one of the world's largest, of crude supplies. At the same time, Nigeria was still exporting crude, (despite all of the theft, that Mele Kyari, the NNPC GMD said we were all involved in and responsible for), while the Dangote refinery was now forced to imports its crude. It gets worse, as the Dangote refinery began to export its refined products, as planned, but likely accelerated by the NNPC's determination to maintain significant control over the local refined market, its goose that lays the golden corrupt egg, off the misery of longsuffering Nigerian indigenes.

2023 - 2024: Tinubu's election seems to be a 'safe choice' compromise for Nigeria's political elite and makers, enablers and stabilizers of the Nigerian state. The reality and structures of the Nigerian State means that governance is almost never about the people, but it is hoped would at least create a dent of the growing and choking poverty.

Like his major rivals[140] in the elections[141], Tinubu comes with a baggage of corruption allegations, which is the norm and not the exception with Nigeria's political elite. What probably put Tinubu ahead of his rivals, is the comfort he provides to the political elite. Including his Vice President, party chairman and his choice for Secretary to the Government, there were about a dozen cabinet level ex-Governors in Tinubu's Government[142]. Speculations about the International comfort [143]with Tinubu led to wild rumors about him being a CIA asset[144]. These realities and speculations may be constraints, shields, or even a leverage for Tinubu. The internal and external power brokers (or stakeholders) will be first in line for proceeds. The key question will be if he can somehow bring impactful governance to impoverished millions of what has become the world's poverty capital and address the structural and fundamental problems.

2023 - Hausa General Abdulrahman Tijani (or Abdourahamane Tchiani, as the French spell his name) joins the coup trend started in Guinea, and overthrows Mohamed Bazoum, the country's elected president, who is popular with France and the West. Niger has significant deposits of Uranium, and hosts (or owns) a US build base.

Also significantly, Niger is about 70% ethnically Hausa, and most of the country's southern 'border' is part of a contiguous Hausa country which continues into Northern Nigeria. This 'border' was created by the plundering criminals in Berlin.

While the suspension of Niger from ECOWAS was understood based on the ECOWAS charter, the plans and threat to invade Niger[145], and cutting the electricity of what is essentially a continuation of the largest constituent country in the Nigerian State was just ineptitude, lack of diligence and a poor understanding of the fabric and makeup of the Nigerian State by Tinubu. It was also horrific that France, a rumored medical destination for Tinubu, seemed to be a driving force for Nigeria's plans, due to threats to the favorable Uranium mining contracts companies like Orano enjoyed in Niger.

Niger, Burkina Faso and Mali eventually voted to leave ECOWAS in February 2024, and the decision was ratified by ECOWAS in December 2024

2023 - 2024: Economic challenges resulting in Naira Collapse (massive devaluation), high inflation, growing poverty and hardship - Tinubu's struggles to implement needed reforms in efficient ways leads to avoidable economic challenges.

Tinubu announced the removal subsidy, but seemingly strengthened NNPC's involvement in the downstream sector, effectively transferring the 'subsidy' from public attention, to NNPC operations, still a drain on the treasury of the peoples and countries of Nigeria.

He then sets up a tax reform committee, which spends the next two years bantering and consulting about tax operations, when the core economic fundamentals of a tax policy can be rolled out in a few days through an executive action. Corporate tax payments can be accelerated by linking them to forex allocations; individual tax payments can be jumpstarted with benign but universal property taxes, and NNPC's now needless position in the downstream petroleum sector can be ended. The policy is always the first step, and the intent can become reality with time and focus but taking more efficient routes results in much quicker wins and less suffering.

2024 - Nigeria's Army Chief, Taoreed Lagbaja dies after a brief illness.

Lagbaja

2024 - Conservative to pessimistic outlooks had the naira crashing by 50% - 70% to the N700 - N800/USD range, post float.[146] However the failure to use available monetary tools (forex) to drive desired fiscal results (taxes) lead to a complete collapse of the naira, with the currency easily breaking the N1000/USD resistance and testing the N2000/USD limits, before an embarrassingly high interest[147] sovereign loan, and a Bloomberg tool to introduce transparency in the market, brought some stability and stemmed the tide.

The damage was already done, as domestic prices on everything from imported products, fuel to food increased four to fivefold (400% to 500%) causing untold levels of pain and hardship, earning President Tinubu the nickname T-Pain, a mocking twist on the name of a popular hip hop artist.

As mentioned in Vol. 1, Nigeria's inflation has largely been forex or exchange rate led, and the economic suffering caused by the naira collapse was not just expected, but pretty much guaranteed.

2024 - Nigeria's political class, and in this case, the national assembly, seems to confirm the perception that the political class is very much aligned with Tinubu by speedingly granting his request to revert the nation to the much-criticized independence era anthem.

2024 - 'Everyone is involved in Oil theft'[148], according to NNPC GMD Mele Kyari, who was retained by Tinubu, bucking the practice where a new NNPC GMD is usually one of the first appointments by a new President. Kyari's admission is merely stating the obvious regarding the fiscal, legal and sometimes institutional arrangements of Nigeria, reinforcing that state (and resource) capture, to the detriment of constituent countries and their peoples, is a fundamental building block of the Nigerian state.

2024 - Aliko Dangote and his team show tremendous resilience to launch the 650,000 b/d refinery, one of the world's largest, and despite the frustrating attempts of NNPC to maintain its badly managed hometurf with both crude supplies and refined products, the refinery was already operating at 50% capacity by December 2024, and making an impact in global refined petroleum markets. Its PMS was already in the neighboring countries of Cameroon, Togo and Ghana, and in other African countries including South Africa and Angola.

The refinery also almost instantly turned Nigeria into a net exporter of Aviation fuel, supplying Airports Spain, England and Iceland. South Korea has however been its largest importer, averaging 23,000 b/d of the industrial fuel product, Naphtha[149].

Sadly a stalemate with the NNPC seems to be heading along the path of 'don't hurt our corruption, and we won't disturb you', and the Dangote refinery may end up being one that largely imports its crude and export its refined products, at least in the 2025 - 2026 medium term.

2024 - In a clear sign of the times, showing the widespread poverty and increasing desperation of people, scores of Nigerians die over a few days at various charity events while trying to collect food items and other freebies in different parts of the country. 35 people, mostly children, were killed in a stampede in Ibadan[150] on December 18th. At least 10 people died while trying to get food and other relief items in Maitama[151], Abuja on December 21st, and on the same day, at least 22 people were killed while trying to get items donated by a philanthropist in Okija, Anambra[152].

The record of history of Nigerian state ends on a sad note in late 2024 as indigenes in various countries that constitute the nation die scrambling for food in various parts of the country. The nation is the poverty capital of the world, with more out-of-school children (now over 20 million) than any other nation and lagging at or near the bottom of most human development indices.

The situation can only get worse for the nation, as currently constituted.

The first volume in this series, 'Poor Nation's Wealth,' examined the economic realities and arrangements that keep the Nigerian state poor and most of the people needlessly impoverished.

This volume, 'The History of Nigeria', examined the global factors that led to the creation of Nigeria, and how it has meandered over the decades, unable to break free from the purpose of its creation, thereby limiting and suppressing its constituent countries, whose potentials cannot be realized within the Nigerian State as designed and structured.

The final book in this series, the 'Confederation of Nigerian States,' will propose solutions to the dire straits in which the people and countries of the Nigerian State find themselves. It is essentially a fire drill handbook, with obvious guidelines and recommendations that will most likely be ignored by the makers, shakers and beneficiaries of Nigeria, but will come in handy when something breaks, and the center can no longer hold.

For a nation that has pretty much gained expertise with tethering on the edge, the increasing stress, weaknesses and failures in several critical areas suggest that it could fall into the category of a failed state sooner than later.

That is when the rescue plan and light that is the 'Confederation of Nigeria States' will shine brightest to guide the countries and peoples of Nigeria from rough waters to safe harbors of prosperity, stability, security and hope.

References

Adegbamigbe, A. (2020, March 5). Retrieved May 19, 2021, from The News Nigeria: https://www.thenewsnigeria.com.ng/2020/03/05/34th-memorial-how-ibb-executed-vatsa-wife-narrates-last-moments/

Akinbode, A. (2020, April 25). *National History: Why the 1992 Gideon Orkar Coup failed*. Retrieved May 19, 2021, from History Ville: https://www.thehistoryville.com/gideon-orkar-coup/

Daily Trust. (2019, March 3). *Reminiscences with Gen Ipoola Alani Akinrinade*. Retrieved from Daily Trust: https://dailytrust.com/reminiscences-with-gen-ipoola-alani-akinrinade

Diamond, L. (1988). The Crises in Western Nigeria. In *Crisis and Conflict in the Western Region, 1962–65. In: Class, Ethnicity and Democracy in Nigeria.* (pp. 93-94). London: Palgrave Macmillan. doi: https://doi.org/10.1007/978-1-349-08080-9_4

Ekine, S. (2010, May 10). *The mysterious disappearance and death of Nigeria's President*. Retrieved May 19, 2021, from The Globe and Mail: https://www.theglobeandmail.com/news/world/the-mysterious-disappearance-and-death-of-nigerias-president/article4318360/

Ekine, S. (2010, May 10). *The mysterious disappearance and death of Nigeria's President*. Retrieved May 19, 2021, from The Globe and Mail: https://www.theglobeandmail.com/news/world/the-mysterious-disappearance-and-death-of-nigerias-president/article4318360/

Obiejesi, K. (2018, July 18). *iNews: Mandela begged Abacha not to execute Ken Saro-Wiwa and companions*. Retrieved May 19, 2020, from International Centre for investigative Reporting: https://www.icirnigeria.org/mandela-begged-abacha-not-to-execute-ken-saro-wiwa-and-companions/

Oduyela, S. (2004, September 17). *Owners of Nigeria - Part 4*. Retrieved from Dawodu.com: https://www.dawodu.com/oduyela9.htm

Oduyela, S. (2004, September 17). *Owners of Nigeria Part 4*. Retrieved May 19, 2021, from Dawodu.com: https://www.dawodu.com/oduyela9.htm

Oduyela, S. (2004, October 21). *Owners of Nigeria Part 8*. Retrieved May 19, 2021, from Dawudu.com: https://www.dawodu.com/oduyela13.htm

Oduyela, S. (2004, October October). *Owners of Nigeria: Part 6*. Retrieved May 19, 2019, from Dawodu.com: https://www.dawodu.com/oduyela11.htm

Omoigui, N. (2021, May 19). *History of Civil-Military Relations in Nigeria (5): the Second Transition (1979-83, Part 2)*. Retrieved from Dawodu.com: https://www.dawodu.com/omoigui7.htm

Omoigui, N. (n.d.). *Col. Dimka's Failed Coup Attempt*. Retrieved May 19, 2021, from Urhobo Waado: http://www.waado.org/nigerdelta/nigeria_facts/militaryrule/omoigui/Dimka-1976.html

Omoigui, N. (n.d.). *Military Rebellion of July 29*. Retrieved May 19, 2021, from Dawodu.com: https://www.dawodu.com/omoigui45.htm

Omoigui, N. (n.d.). *Murtala Ramat Muhammed (1938-1976)*. Retrieved May 19, 2021, from Dawodu.com: https://dawodu.com/murtala3.htm

Oredein, O. (1985, April 10). *Three Nigerians shot for drug possession*. Retrieved from United Press International: https://www.upi.com/Archives/1985/04/10/Three-Nigerians-shot-for-drug-possession/7864481957200/

Siollun, M. (n.d.). *The Rollercoaster Life of Murtala Muhammed*. Retrieved May 19, 2021, from Dawodu.com: https://www.dawodu.com/siollun2.htm

The New York Times. (1976, March 13). *Nigeria Executes 30 for Coup Role*. Retrieved from The New York Times: https://www.nytimes.com/1976/03/13/archives/nigeria-executes-30-for-coup-role-exdefense-minister-among-them.html

Walker, A. (2016, February 4). *World News*. Retrieved May 19, 2021, from The Guardian: https://www.theguardian.com/world/2016/feb/04/join-us-or-die-birth-of-boko-haram

Watch, H. R. (2002, April 1). *Nigeria: Soldiers Massacre Civilians in Revenge Attack in Benue State*. Retrieved May 19, 2021, from Human

Rights Watch: https://www.hrw.org/news/2001/10/25/nigeria-soldiers-massacre-civilians-revenge-attack-benue-state

1 The West Australian. July 5, 1899

2 The Aukland Star, Wednesday, July 5, 1899

3 By United States government - U.S. Army Area Handbook for Nigeria. Second Edition, March 1964, Public Domain, https://commons.wikimedia.org/w/index.php?curid=93868318

4 A similar pattern emerged with a long lag between Europe's first declaration of the ownership of Africa at Torcesillas and the relatively quick occupation of the continent following the identification of the Malaria parasite.

5 The suggestion that the Fulbe clans that took over Hausa Country are a 'homeless race' is untrue, and shows the ignorance and limitations of many European 'experts' on Africa, including those who in pursuit of their fleeting needs and interests at a point in time, drew the maps of 'Nigeria' and other African Countries in the criminal gathering in Berlin. These limitations and lack of contextual knowledge are probably even more pronounced with those who set the global agenda within which Africa and Africans operate.

6 Rabih Az Zubair killed Shehu El-Kanemi and ruled Borno for 7 years before losing his life to the French in battle.

7 Curtin P.D., Death by migration: Europe's encounter with the tropical world in the nineteenth century. 1989: Cambridge University Press. [DOI] [PubMed] [Google Scholar], https://pmc.ncbi.nlm.nih.gov/articles/PMC10021769/

8 https://www.immunopaedia.org.za/immunology/special-focus-area/4-immunity-to-malaria/

9 Rawley J.A., The Port of London and the Eighteenth-Century Slave Trade: Historians, Sources, and a Reappraisal. African Economic History, 1980

10 Laveran A., Discours d'ouverture de la première séance de la Société de pathologie exotique le 22 janvier 1908. Bull Soc Pathol Exot, 1908. 1: p. 1–8.

11 Part of the proceeds of this book will be used to raise a fund to reimburse this blood money to the English Parliament.

12 http://www.thelongridersguild.com/clapperton.htm

13 https://www.worldhistory.org/Oyo_Empire/

14 Also known as Lucumi, Aku, Oku, Nago, Anago, Yoruba, or by evolutions of their traditional religion including Regla de Ocha (religion of the orisha's), candomble, and santeria.

15 Ajayi Crowther's account of how he was enslaved. From various sources online including https://thenigerialawyer.com/ajayi-crowthers-182-year-old-letter-how-i-was-captured-sold-into-slavery/

16 No pun intended. These statements are attributed to men held in high esteem and credited with significant intellectual achievement.

17 The death rate of the slave march across the sahara was reported to be sometimes as high as 8 or 9 out of 10.

18 https://guardian.ng/features/re-introduction-of-history-and-matters-arising/

19 https://brittlepaper.com/2013/02/love-lies-empire-lugard/

20 Rt. Hon Gentleman, Page 651

21 Honor in African History, Page 314

22 Author uses Afeire or Afere instead of the popularly accepted slur and exonym for the confederated sub-ethnicities primarily located in the Southwest of Nigeria and their related ethnic nationalities.

23 https://www.vanguardngr.com/2020/01/ojukwu-banjo-conceived-what-could-have-been-first-coup-in-1964-gowon/

24 https://thenewsnigeria.com.ng/2021/01/15/55-years-of-nigerias-1st-coup-what-british-intelligence-officials-wrote-about-it/

25 Some suggestion of a personal dispute stemming from a love triangle has been stated as the reason for Lt. Col. Unegbe's murder.

26 https://www.vanguardngr.com/2017/06/meet-first-30-nigerian-military-officers-before-1960/

27 This can be taken to include the so-called Yoruba areas in Nigeria and 'Benin' Republic, and the related Igala, Edo, Esan and Itskeri Countries

28 Yoruba Leaders Call for Withdrawal of Northern Troops From Western Region | December 1966 (https://www.youtube.com/watch?v=iNs7f_aH2_M)

29 Another foremost Nigerian Military Historian, Dr. Nowa Omoigui suggests Rtd Col. Garba Dada (Paiko) died much earlier, at some point before 2003.

30 Some refer to 'Aure Paiko' as Operation Araba. Araba is the Hausa word for separation or partition, and this was the objective of the plotters.

31 https://guardian.ng/news/awos-wife-convinced-him-to-join-my-government-says-gowon/

32 There has been some decades-long controversy over whether these areas (including the Ikwere areas of Rivers) are Igbo or just Igbo speaking.

33 https://www.vanguardngr.com/2020/05/anioma-v-igbo/

34 The name BenDel state from Benin and Delta provinces was adopted in 1966. Babangida in 1991, separated Bendel into 2 states, and included Warri in Delta State, while choosing Asaba, the hometown of his wife Maryam, as the capital of the State. Benin City remained the Capital of the new Edo State.

35 This cannot be proven, but 'everyone' believed the Alaafin diabolically killed Bode Thomas, and the Monarch did little to correct the impression.

36 https://www.news24.com/news24/africa/news/us-court-battle-gives-clues-to-nigerian-arms-scandal-20170518

37 https://www.history.org.uk/historian/resource/10169/legacies-of-the-cement-armada

38 https://www.euromoney.com/article/b1f5w54yw0gxzh/the-extra-ordinary-nigerian-jumbo

39 (Omoigui, Military Rebellion of July 29, n.d.)

40 (Omoigui, Murtala Ramat Muhammed (1938-1976), n.d.)

41 (Siollun, n.d.)

42 https://www.vanguardngr.com/2015/08/how-corruption-hit-civil-service-asiodu/

43 https://www.sunnewsonline.com/murtalaobasanjo-stopped-nige-rias-march-to-greatness-phillip-asiodu/

44 (Omoigui, Col. Dimka's Failed Coup Attempt, n.d.)

45 (Omoigui, Col. Dimka's Failed Coup Attempt, n.d.)

46 (The New York Times, 1976)

47 (Omoigui, Military Rebellion of July 29, n.d.)

48 (Oduyela S., 2004)

49 (Daily Trust, 2019)

50 (Omoigui, History of Civil-Military Relations in Nigeria (5): the Second Transition (1979-83, Part 2), 2021)

51 https://climate-diplomacy.org/case-studies/conflict-between-fulani-and-toubou-niger

52 https://www.legit.ng/1102783-atiku-account-53-suitcases-saga-imported-nigeria.html

53 https://www.theguardian.com/music/2004/aug/15/popandrock5

54 https://www.spin.com/featured/fela-kuti-july-1986-interview-fela-freed/

55 https://onlinenigeria.com/nm/templates/?a=12357

56 (Oredein, 1985)

57 https://rainbownigeria.com/2020/11/28/ibrahim-babangida-regime/

58 (Adegbamigbe, 2020)

59 We let justice take its course on Dele Giwa - Ibrahim Babangida on Straight Talk with Kadaria 44e https://www.youtube.com/watch?v=ziyyW-QP8fk&t=187s

60 (Diamond, 1988)

61 (Akinbode, 2020)

62 https://www.vanguardngr.com/2018/05/gideon-orkars-madness-another-april-anniversary-2/

63 (Oduyela S., Owners of Nigeria Part 4, 2004)

64 https://www.thenewsnigeria.com.ng/2021/06/11/june-12-annulment-why-i-made-sure-abacha-also-ruled-nigeria-babangida/

65 The exception will be for the first wife in a polygamous marriage.

66 Channels TV YouTube Video - MKO Abiola speaks about his plans, vision for Nigeria.

67 https://www.chicagotribune.com/news/ct-xpm-1998-06-09-9806090183-story.html

68 (Oduyela S., Owners of Nigeria: Part 6, 2004)

69 https://www.independent.co.uk/news/world/africa/ken-saro-wiwa-was-framed-secret-evidence-shows-2151577.html

70 (Obiejesi, 2018)

71 (Oduyela S., Owners of Nigeria Part 8, 2004)

72 https://www.vanguardngr.com/2017/11/ekwuemes-words-marble/

73 https://www.vanguardngr.com/2016/05/abacha-never-stole/

74 Daily Trust, Feb 16, 2020

75 (Watch, 2002)

76 https://www.vanguardngr.com/2019/10/26bn-diaspora-remittances-where-are-the-dollars-2/

77 https://www.premiumtimesng.com/business/business-news/398151-three-refineries-lost-n1-6trillion-in-5-years-says-nnpc-audit-report.html

78 https://www.thisdaylive.com/index.php/2019/12/17/nnpcs-refineries-record-losses-for-nine-consecutive-months/

79 https://www.thisdaylive.com/index.php/2019/10/18/report-nnpc-spent-396-33m-on-refineries-tam-in-four-years/

80 https://www.vanguardngr.com/2015/07/how-yaradua-was-pressurised-to-revert-refineries-sold-to-dangote-obasanjo/

81 https://punchng.com/yaradua-was-wrong-to-have-reversed-sale-of-refineries-by-obasanjo-ex-nnpc-executive-director-ihetu/

82 https://www.reuters.com/article/nigeria-refineries-idUKL1944935220070719

83 https://face2faceafrica.com/article/how-350000-people-have-been-killed-due-to-boko-haram-scourge-in-nigeria

84 (Walker, 2016)

85 (Ekine, The mysterious disappearance and death of Nigeria's President, 2010)

86 https://www.premiumtimesng.com/news/headlines/204809-pressured-squander-18bn-excess-crude-saving-jonathan.html

87 https://www.ft.com/content/0a7935ae-ca97-11df-a860-00144feab49a

88 https://www.reuters.com/article/ozatp-nigeria-ibori-20100422-idAFJOE63L02W20100422

89 https://pmnewsnigeria.com/2010/10/08/group-wants-kaita-tried-for-treason/

90 https://www.sunnewsonline.com/wanted-northern-president-2011-instead-jonathan-adamu-ciroma/

91 https://pmnewsnigeria.com/2011/04/21/northern-riots-100-bodies-recovered-jonathan-orders-probe/

92 https://www.vanguardngr.com/2011/05/post-election-violence-n5m-for-each-slain-corps-members-family/

93   https://www.vanguardngr.com/2012/05/2015-ll-be-bloody-if-buhari/

94   https://www.thisdaylive.com/index.php/2021/06/16/buhari-approves-jobs-for-2011-post-election-violence-victims-families/

95   https://www.vanguardngr.com/2014/09/amaechi-laments-harassment-supporters-police/

96   https://www.modernghana.com/news/470735/amaechi-cp-mbu-and-politics-of-security-in-rivers.html

97 https://www.thecable.ng/amaechi-arrested-detained-in-ekiti

98   https://punchng.com/amaechi-had-problem-with-patience-not-me-jonathan/

99   https://www.vanguardngr.com/2017/05/jonathan-awarded-pre-shipment-inspection-contracts-72hrs-exiting-power-contractor/

100 https://www.premiumtimesng.com/news/headlines/175497-full-text-video-nsa-sambo-dasukis-famous-presentation-chatham-house-london.html

101 https://punchng.com/news/north-reps-forced-jonathan-to-sack-azazi-defence-minister-investigation/

102   https://thenationonlineng.net/buhari-faults-clampdown-on-boko-haram-members/

103   https://www.pulse.ng/news/politics/buhari-ministers-are-just-noisemakers-like-politicians-president-says/jv3zck3

104 https://www.theguardian.com/world/2015/sep/30/nigerian-president-muhammadu-buhari-to-become-oil-minister-in-own-cabinet

105   https://dailypost.ng/2017/10/30/81-100-appointees-president-buhari-northern-region-see-full-list/

106   https://www.premiumtimesng.com/news/top-news/189383-buhari-sued-over-lopsided-appointments.html

107   https://www.theguardian.com/world/2015/dec/16/nigerian-army-killings-of-shia-muslims-to-be-investigated

108 https://punchng.com/el-zakzaky-1886-children-orphaned-200-arrested-since-zaria-massacre-says-imn/

109 Long term Chadian strongman, Idris Deby was killed in a battle with CACT rebels in the 'Kanem' region of Chad. A spokesman for the FACT rebels had the same surname as Nigeria's special envoy to Chad on

the crisis. The envoy is a long-term Nigerian power broker of Kanuri origins.

110   https://www.vanguardngr.com/2019/05/kanuris-influence-on-buhari/

111   https://dailypost.ng/2021/07/27/fgs-silence-on-insecurity-a-continuation-of-1804-jihadist-movement-ortom/

112   https://www.reuters.com/article/us-nigeria-politics-idUSKBN1KS0R1

113 https://guardian.ng/news/outrage-as-buhari-removes-dss-chief/

114 https://www.bbc.co.uk/news/world-africa-34973872

115   https://www.premiumtimesng.com/news/headlines/369206-u-s-lawmakers-write-nigerias-agf-malami-over-sowore.html

116 *Murtala removed Justice Teslim Elias from as Chief Justice following the coup against Gowon in 1975*

117 https://www.economist.com/middle-east-and-africa/2019/02/02/nigerias-president-sacks-the-chief-justice-weeks-before-an-election

118   https://www.thecable.ng/promoted-behold-the-62-failed-2015-election-campaign-promises-of-muhammadu-buhari-and-apc

119   https://www.vanguardngr.com/2021/07/nigeria-witnessing-the-epilogue/

120   https://www.vanguardngr.com/2021/06/i-was-not-invited-arrested-quizzed-by-dss-sheikh-gumi/

121   https://www.legit.ng/1416930-list-names-10-officers-died-alongside-general-attahiru-plane-crash.html

122   https://www.premiumtimesng.com/news/top-news/469999-buhari-postpones-london-medical-trip.html

123   https://www.theguardian.com/world/2016/jun/07/muhammadu-buhari-nigeria-ear-infection-medical-treatment-uk

124   https://www.premiumtimesng.com/news/headlines/477336-timeline-buhari-has-spent-200-days-in-uk-for-treatment-since-assuming-office.html

125   https://www.vanguardngr.com/2017/10/urgent-aisha-buhari-calls-for-probe-of-state-house-medical-centre-over-poor-facilities/

126 https://punchng.com/breaking-abduction-kaduna-orders-closure-of-13-schools/?utm_medium=Social&utm_source=Twit-

ter&amp&utm_medium=Social&utm_source=Twitter&__twitter_impr
ession=true

127 https://dailypost.ng/2021/08/10/plateau-massacre-buhari-orders-military-to-kill-illegal-weapon-holders/

128   https://www.vanguardngr.com/2021/08/breaking-gunmen-invade-jos-north-community-in-fresh-attack-over-30-killed/

129   https://independent.ng/plateau-killings-nans-group-evacu-ate-279-fct-students-from-jos/

130 https://punchng.com/parents-lament-as-kaduna-confirms-abduc-tion-of-39-students/

131 https://punchng.com/breaking-kaduna-forestry-college-students-released-56-days-after/

132   https://www.channelstv.com/2021/04/27/abducted-pregnant-student-others-call-for-help-in-new-video-released-by-bandits/

133 https://thenationonlineng.net/underground-economy/

134   https://www.barrons.com/news/guinea-closes-borders-with-guinea-bissau-senegal-ahead-of-vote-01601390704

135 https://www.africanews.com/2020/10/19/i-won-cellou-diallo-de-clares-himself-victorious-in-guinea-election//

136   https://punchng.com/Business-booms-for-naira-traders-as-bankers-collusion-worsens-scarcity/

137 https://www.aljazeera.com/news/2023/2/28/nigeria-presidential-election-results-2023

138 https://punchng.com/nigeria-imported-2-25bn-fuel-from-malta-report/

139   https://www.thecable.ng/dangote-some-nnpc-personnel-oil-traders-have-blending-plant-in-malta/

140 https://www.nbcnews.com/id/wbna13170084

141   https://www.vanguardngr.com/2009/07/alleged-n250m-anam-bra-money-police-launches-fresh-investigation/

142 https://www.thecable.ng/wike-oyetola-el-rufai-nine-former-gover-nors-on-tinubus-ministerial-list/

143   https://www.occrp.org/en/news/us-blocks-records-on-nigerian-presidents-alleged-drug-ties

144   https://www.pulse.ng/articles/news/us-court-upholds-cias-posi-tion-on-bola-tinubus-past-records-2024111911405928394

145 https://punchng.com/niger-dhq-directs-service-chiefs-to-compile-war-items-ecowas-lawmakers-divided/

146 https://www.thecable.ng/naira-to-appreciate-settle-at-n600-1-in-coming-months-says-jp-morgan/

147 While Nigeria's Eurobond debt was five times oversubscribed, it came with high interest (coupon) rates of 9.625 and 10.375%, compared to the rates of other African countries including Benin (8.375%), Senegal (7.75%) and (7.85% and 8.35%)

148 https://dailytrust.com/everyone-involved-in-oil-theft-says-nnpcl/

149 https://www.spglobal.com/commodity-insights/en/news-research/latest-news/crude-oil/112224-feature-refiners-brace-for-margin-pain-as-nigerias-dangote-refinery-scales-up

150 https://www.aljazeera.com/news/2024/12/19/nigeria-stampede-at-youth-festival-causes-multiple-deaths

151 https://abcnews.go.com/International/wireStory/13-people-including-children-die-stampedes-nigeria-christmas-117013698

152 https://www.barrons.com/news/south-nigeria-crowd-stampede-toll-rises-to-22-police-8c9c3f16